Dreams, Bright and Dark

Curator: Jerry Cullum

Exhibition at StudioSwan

Atlanta, Georgia

June 9 – July 13, 2007

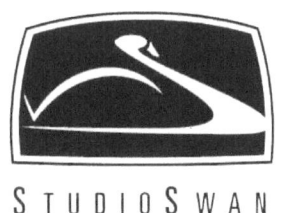

STUDIOSWAN

Serenbe · 9077 Selborne Lane · Palmetto · Georgia 30268 · (770)463-9440 · www.studioswan.com

Designed by Mina Porell and Leigh Rothman

Library of Congress Cataloging-in-Publication Data. Printed in Atlanta

Swanston Jr., Thomas

ISBN: 978-0-6151-4890-8

We would like to acknowledge and thank Jody Fausett, Meta Gary, Heather Hartman, Sonya Jilani, Emily Karcher, Shana Robbins, and Amanda Palmer for capturing their dreams and sharing them. Special thanks to Jerry Cullum who eloquently describes the relationship between an artist and their dreams. We would also like to thank Whitespace, Atlanta for allowing StudioSwan to exhibit the works of Jody Fausett whom they represent exclusively.

Cover artwork: Meta Gary, *Of Course Who Could Be Expected to Remember Everything,* acrylic and graphite on wood, 24" x 48", 2006

Contents

Jerry Cullum

Dreams, Bright and Dark

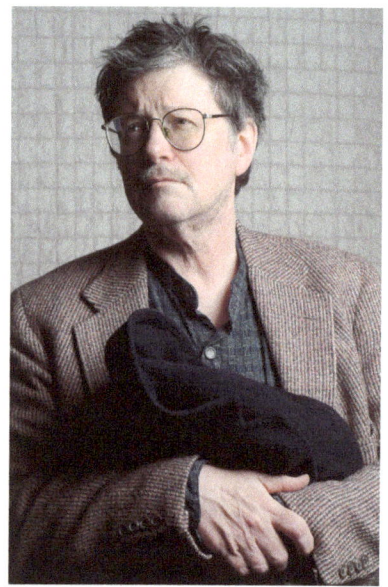

I like to take note of dream narratives. People who once would have at most written their dreams in notes to friends now post them on weblogs for the whole planet to enjoy, (There are whole discussion boards devoted to the topic, but the random postings are better.)

Sometimes the tales are mundane, but more often they are genuinely mysterious: caverns in Egypt where workers empty out pails full of blood while keeping their eyes closed, or life in the Athens of 1945 that nevertheless is also the Greece of antiquity. As is the way of dreams, daily life intrudes: the way out of Egypt leads onto a train in Finland.

It is all very strange, and no surprise then that friends of the novelist John Crowley should have undertaken a typology of dreams, discussed for a while on the crowleycrow LiveJournal and then shunted off to a separate site.

But it is a typology of themes, not of meaning; for the current trend is to think that dreams are, on the whole, meaningless, the mind's attempt to make sense of random scraps by weaving a narrative out of nonsense.

On the other hand, that is how some people define the business of making one's way through daily life. And the narrative of dreams has often seemed to embody, at least upon waking, portentous insight such as comes from that part of us that knows more than we know in our waking moments. (Those who assert the meaninglessness of dreams also remind us that ninety per cent of our activity takes place without conscious awareness.)

For the world of Greece and Rome, of course, dreams were divided into the true visions emerging through the gate of horn, and the delusions exiting through the ivory gate. And the business of the seer was to know which was which.

Richard A. Underwood, a scholar whose achievement was too little noted in his lifetime, once wrote, in an essay called "Hermes and Hermeneutics," that the world of myth lived again wherever human beings dreamed, and *marked* their dreams. If so, then the archetypes live anew on the Web. For dreams have seldom been so marked and recounted, even though the depth psychology in which Underwood put his hope has receded from popular awareness in the age of abundant antidepressant medications.

Who remembers the dream interpretation of either Freud or Jung, beyond the students of literature? Well, artists remain enchanted by both, sometimes both at once, and some writers mine the great essays of European psychologists as much as the mythic trove of tales assembled by Joseph Campbell.

Dreams are our personal myths, even if we make the details up when we awaken. Joseph Campbell noticed that the world's origin myths included the phase of dreamless sleep, but it is in the dream that the stories and images start.

William Butler Yeats named that sphere of personal imagination "the foul rag-and-bone shop of the heart." But he did so only to point out that it is from the scrap heap of personal hope that both individual vision and collective rebirths have historically arisen, just as Yeats saw when the great tales of the Irish gods abandoned him. ("The Circus Animals' Desertion")

Ernst Bloch saw in his densely poetic philosophy that there were dreams of the day that were as good as dreams of the night: or better, because the dreamers knew what it was they were dreaming. "The daydreamer often follows will-o'-the-wisps, get led astray. But he [or she] is not asleep and does not sink back down with the mist." (*The Principle of Hope*, I, 78)

The artists in this exhibition are dreamers of personal dreams, not tellers or creators of collective stories, and yet their hopes and wishes are in a code that speaks to us even as it remains most deeply their own.

Their dreams are a mixture of bright and dark, and there is no Joseph or Daniel to interpret the dreams for us as those heroes of the Holy Scriptures once did for imperial monarchs. There is, indeed, not even a Wise Old Man out of Carl Jung's personal mythos: the archetypes here are oblique, though they give us pleasure.

Thus the viewer is invited to engage in the dreams of day as an individual action: to dream, not the myth or story, but the dream itself onward.

Jody Fausett

Smoke from another Fire

Jody Fausett's work deals with human vulnerability, the self-construction of facades, the rites of ownership and the creation of personal icons as representations of who and what we are. He looks at the world as he sees it, a series of stages and occasions created by all humanity in the common walk of life to mark occasions or simply, to define who and what we are. If his viewpoint seems to represent a tableau then he has achieved exactly what he set out to do; to define that very moment when, despite all our efforts to command personal perfection, we are shown at our most human and most vulnerable.

We desire wholeness. We will paint, present and beautify ourselves to create the illusion of what we know as self. In the privacy of our homes we rewrite the confusion that is our secret existence and emerge each day reborn. For an instant we are the best that we can be and from that instance the beginning of our devolution resumes.

Jody attempts not only to reflect upon the inherent illusions of life but also to celebrate the uniqueness that we as individuals bring to it through use of "props", our carefully chosen costumes and fetish objects serving both as a barrier to bitter reality and a balm for it. He seeks the ordinary and then looks deeper to define the extraordinary in all of us.

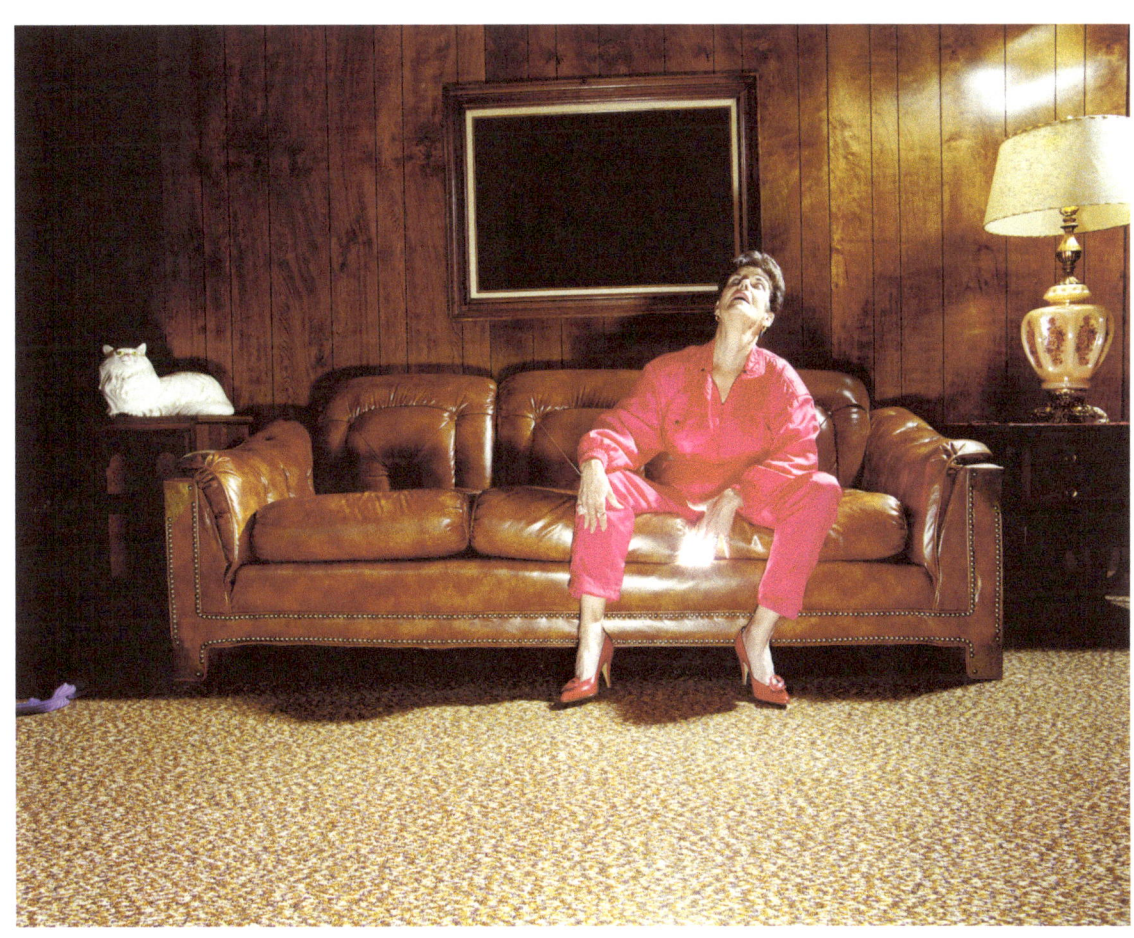

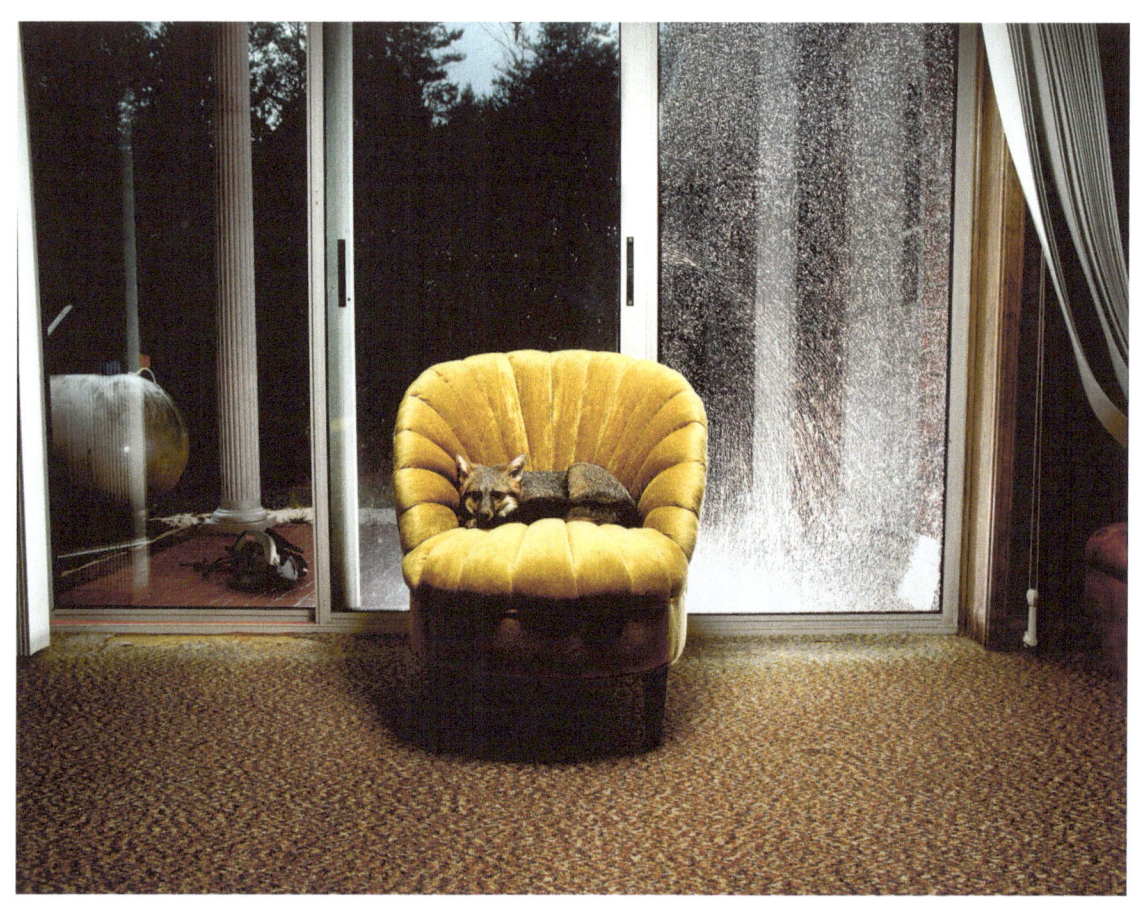

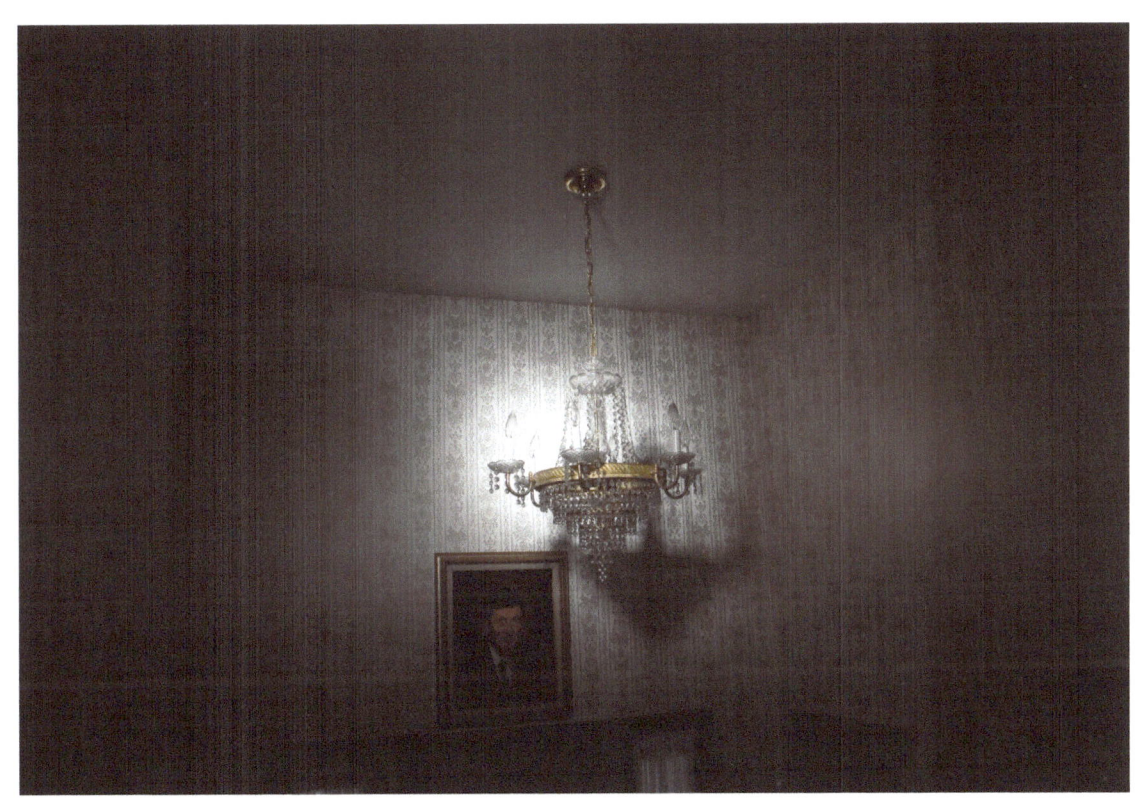

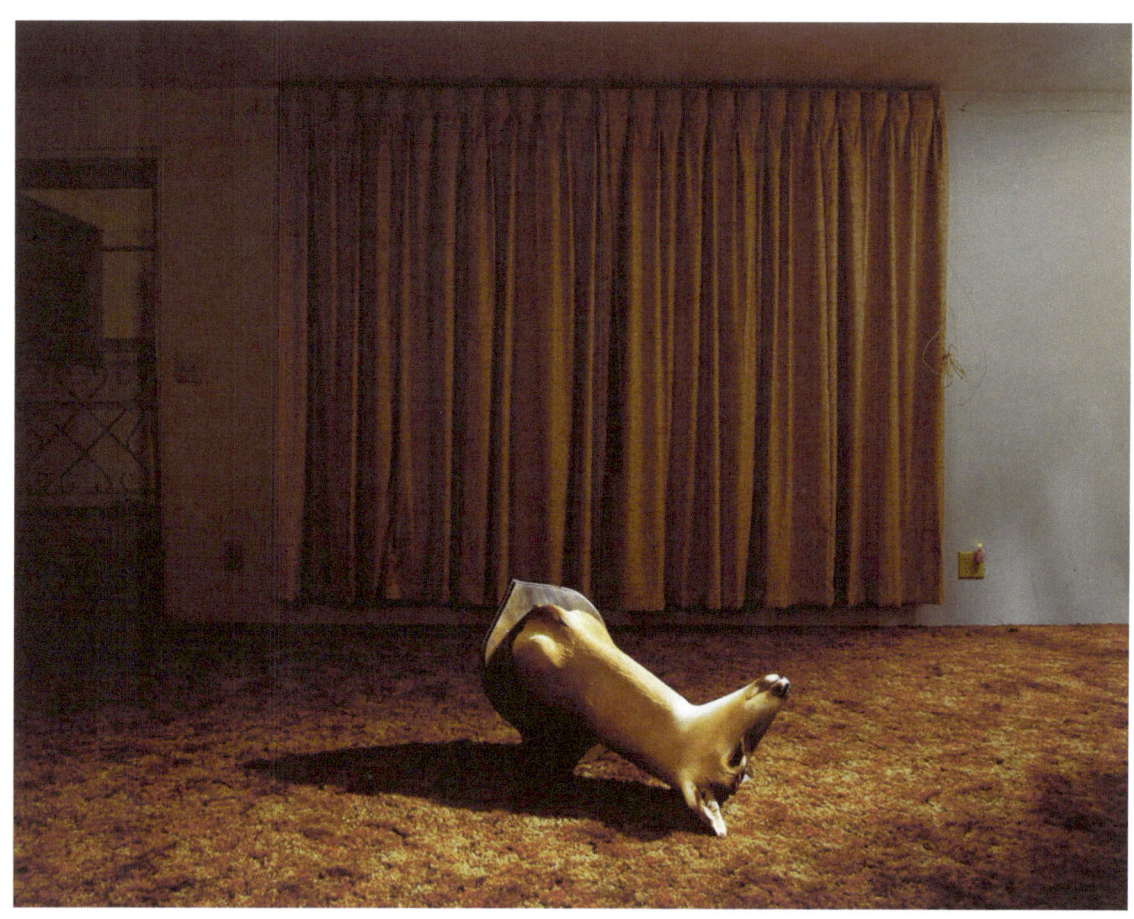

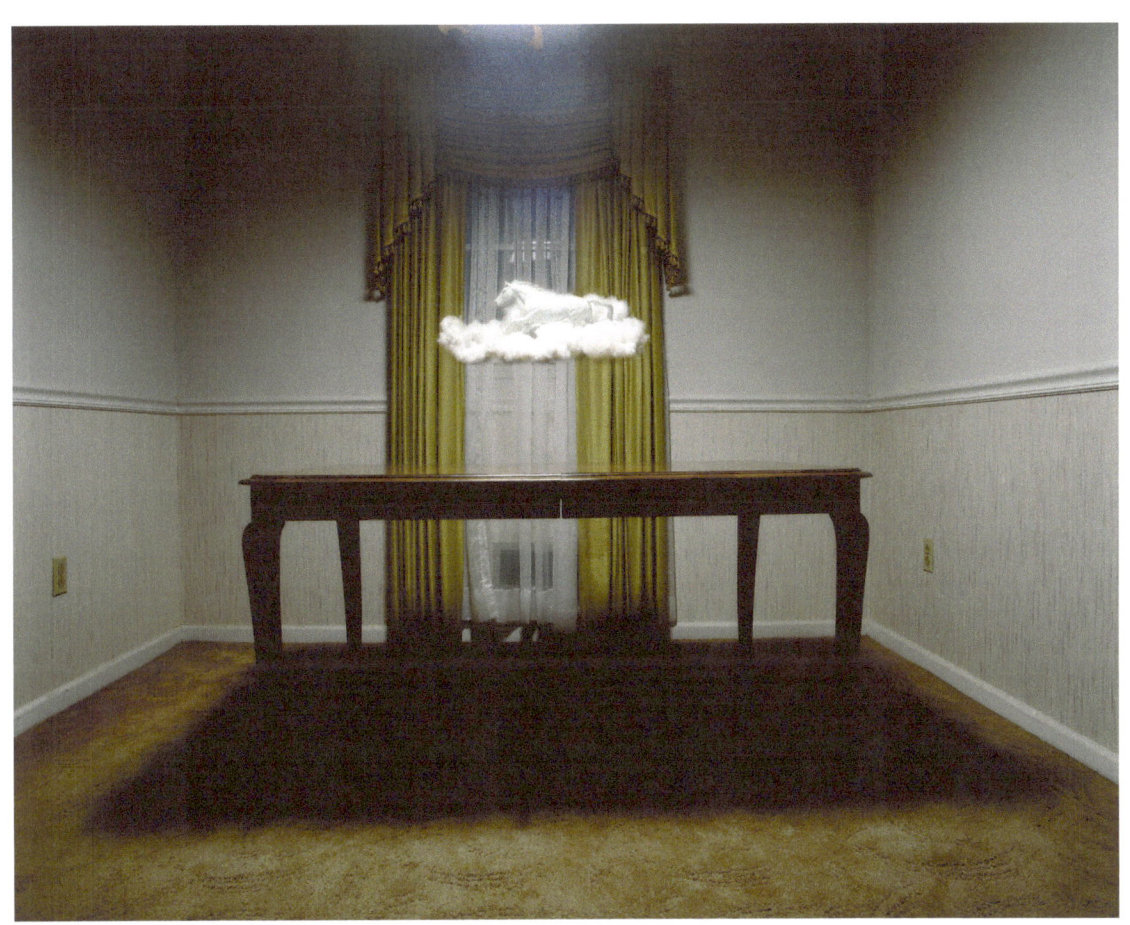

Meta Gary

Astral Menagerie

I have dreams about animals. The animals are not always key components in the plots of my dreams. Sometimes they are in the periphery but they are always there and with a closer intimacy and mutual understanding than in our relationships in waking life. In my paintings, I explore these interactions and general relationships or blurred boundaries that exist between humans and animals.

In most of my paintings, I incorporate a stencil technique by making one-time-use contact paper stencils to achieve smooth edges and isolated color. I paint on untreated, exposed wood as a visual contrast to the flat, colorful shapes of my images. Since wood is an organic, living material, it exists with inherent patterns and personality that need no manipulation and compliment the concrete images applied to them. This graphic style, softened by the organic element brings a simple, innocent aesthetic to my paintings.

While working on this body on work, I saw a program about the speculated interpretations of ancient cave paintings. The consensus is that cave paintings, which most often incorporate animals or humans interacting or combined with animals, were painted by shamen following a ritual trance. In the trances, called astral travels, the shaman's spirit leaves his body and travels to meet animal spirits, who were believed to offer the wisdom necessary to a shaman's healing or leadership powers. When he returned to the waking conscious life, the shaman painted what he saw in his "dreams" onto the walls of the caves, which were believed to be a living element and earthly component of the portal to the spirit world. The distinct parallel between the primitive shaman's work and my own is the inspiration for the title of this body of work.

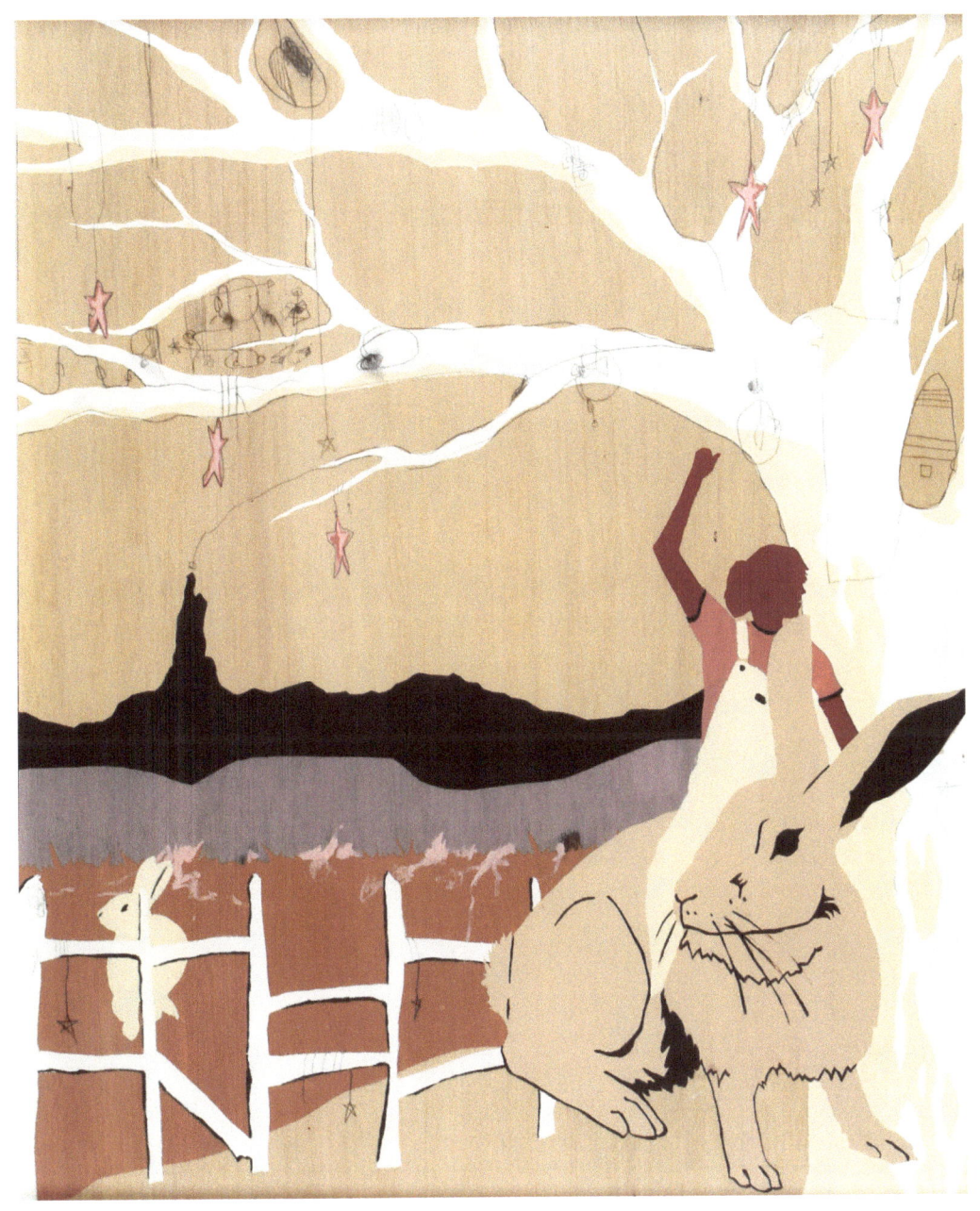

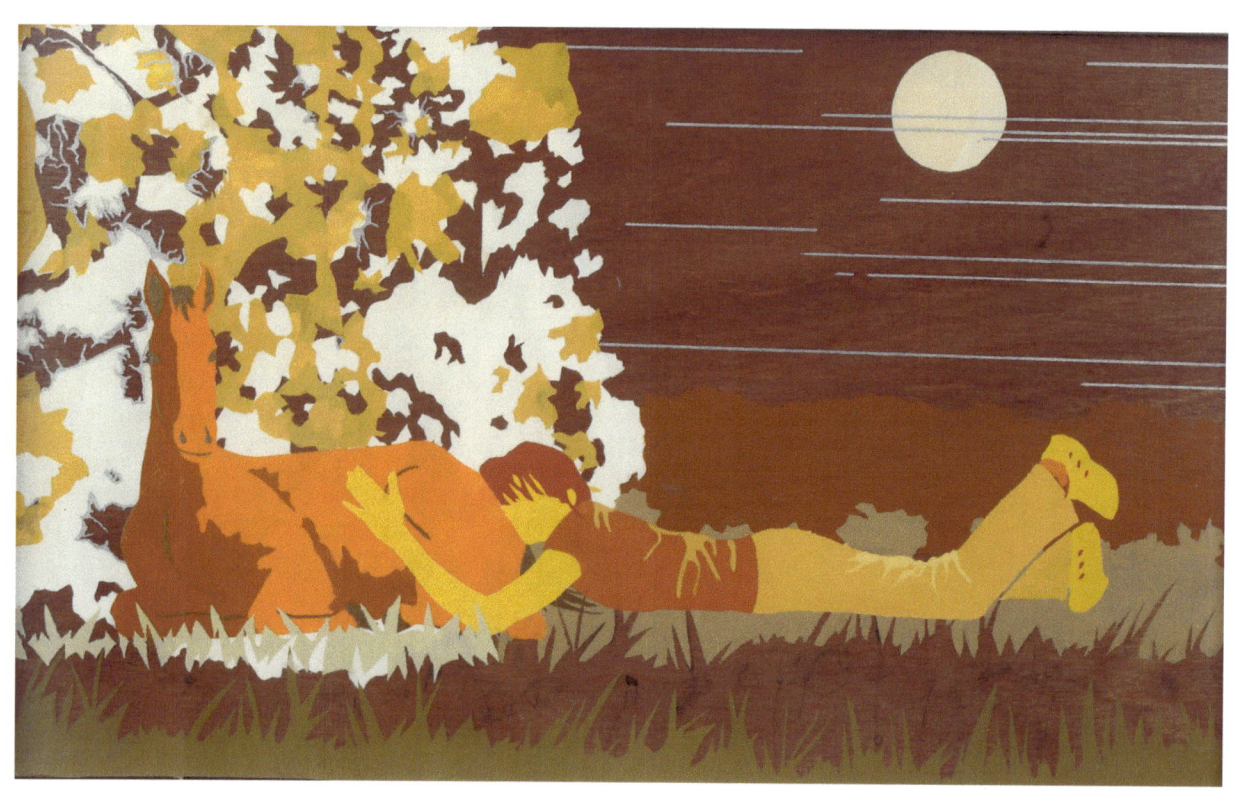

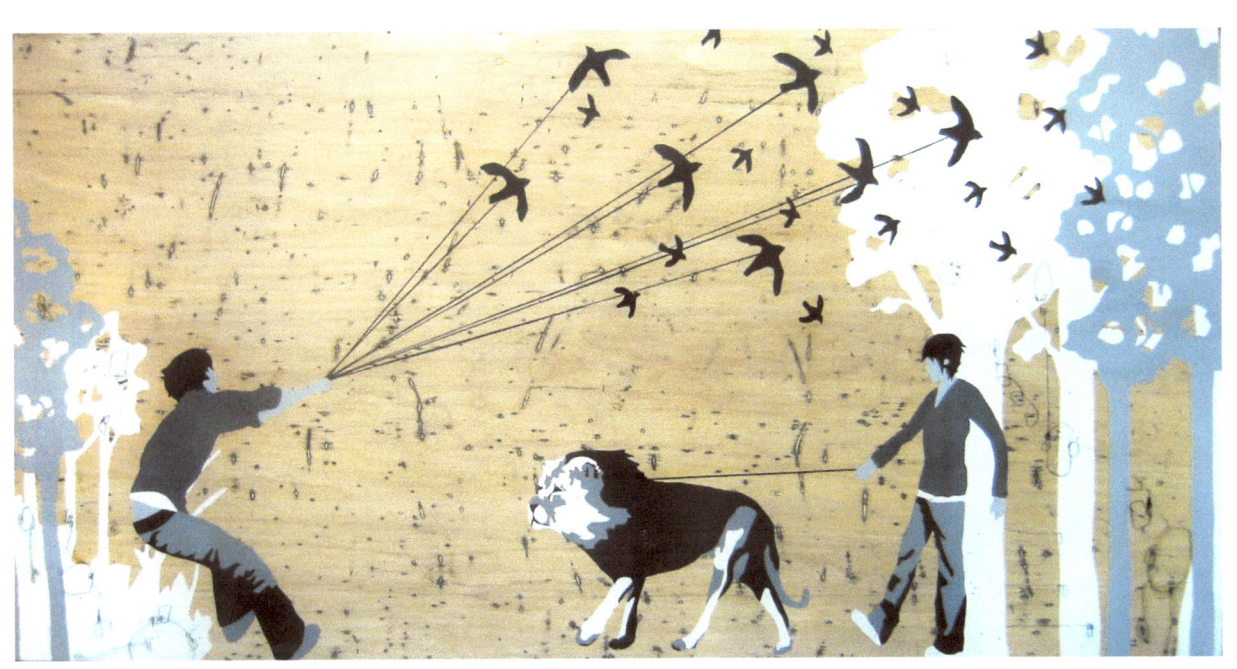

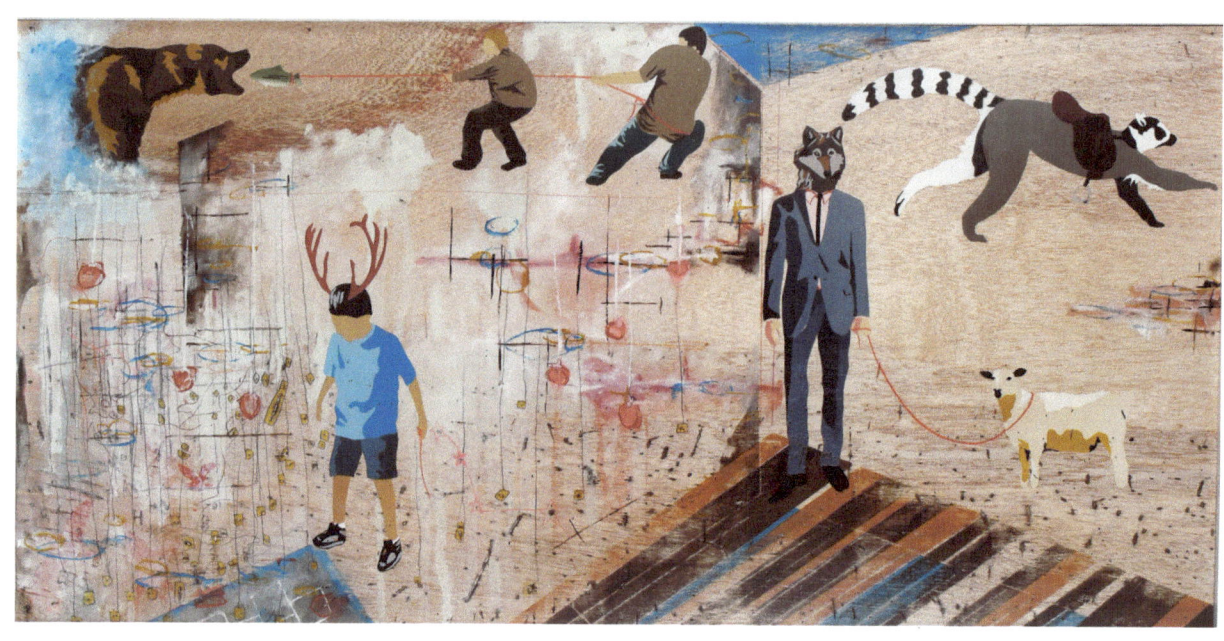

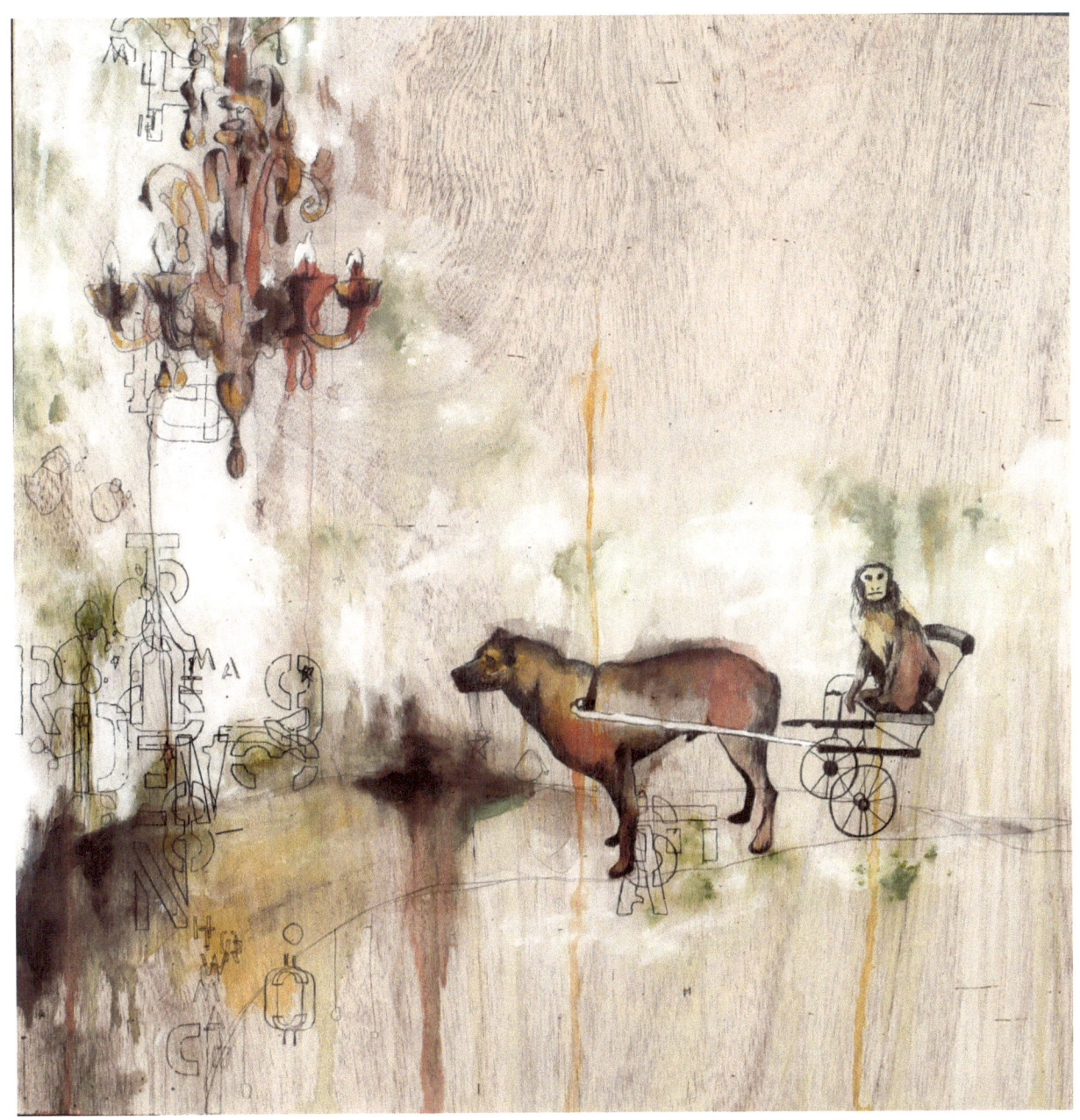

Heather Hartman

Scenes of cosmic creation and destruction exist not only in the far reaches of space, but also in the abstract spaces of the mind. It is in these intangible places that internal conditions collide with external stimuli, creating the sublime experience. The residue of these events lingers in a kind of mental landscape. This body of work is based on my memory of specific moments of epiphany and the metal states surrounding them. They are about the dream I can't quite remember, or that strange apparition that passes through my peripheral vision. The paintings contain the remains of passed events, and the ingredients of future happenings. They address the unexpected moments of awareness in which all things are neutralized. Destruction is beautiful, chaos is peaceful, and the trauma of everyday existence seems perfectly in line with the rhythm of the cosmos. Time stands still, allowing us to see a situation in its full scope with all its infinite possibilities. These moments are often triggered by mundane phenomena and are too frequently passed over because they lie in the periphery of our existence. The way light subtly plays upon a wall or the sparkle of a broken beer bottle on the street can cause an existential realization if we are open and sensitive to these possibilities. By conveying my own experience of awareness, I wish to refocus the viewer's attention on the quiet wonders and mysteries in their own lives.

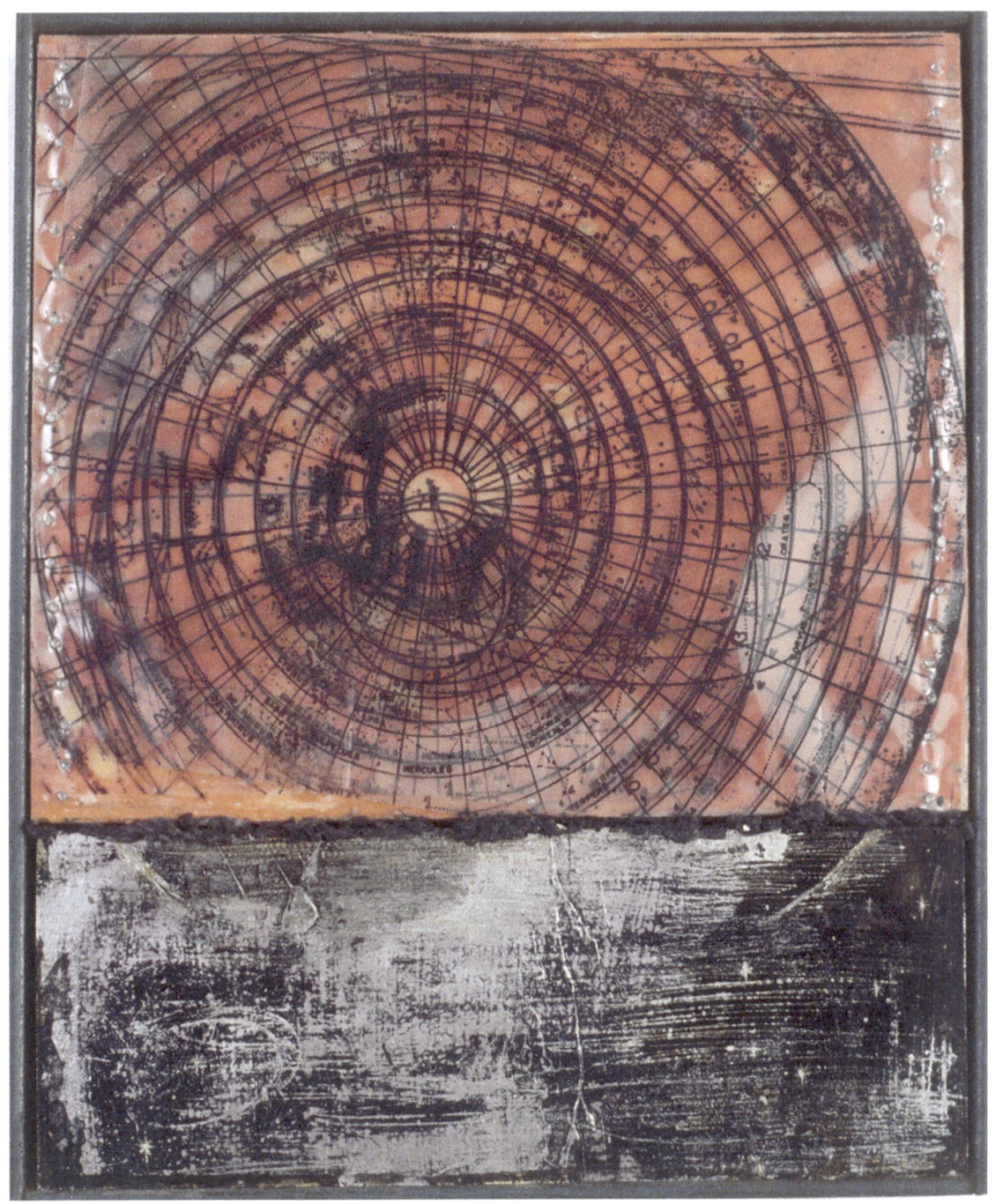

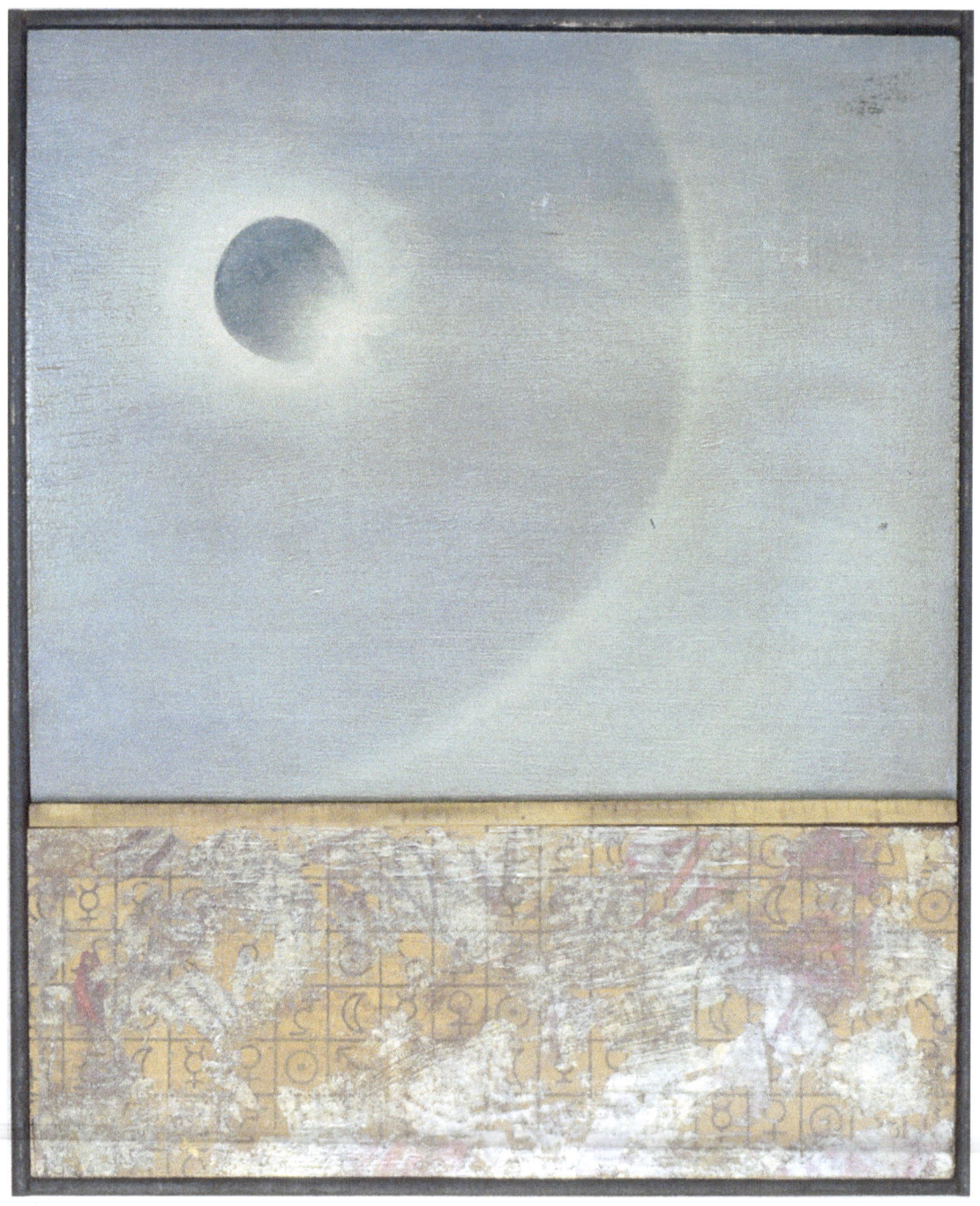

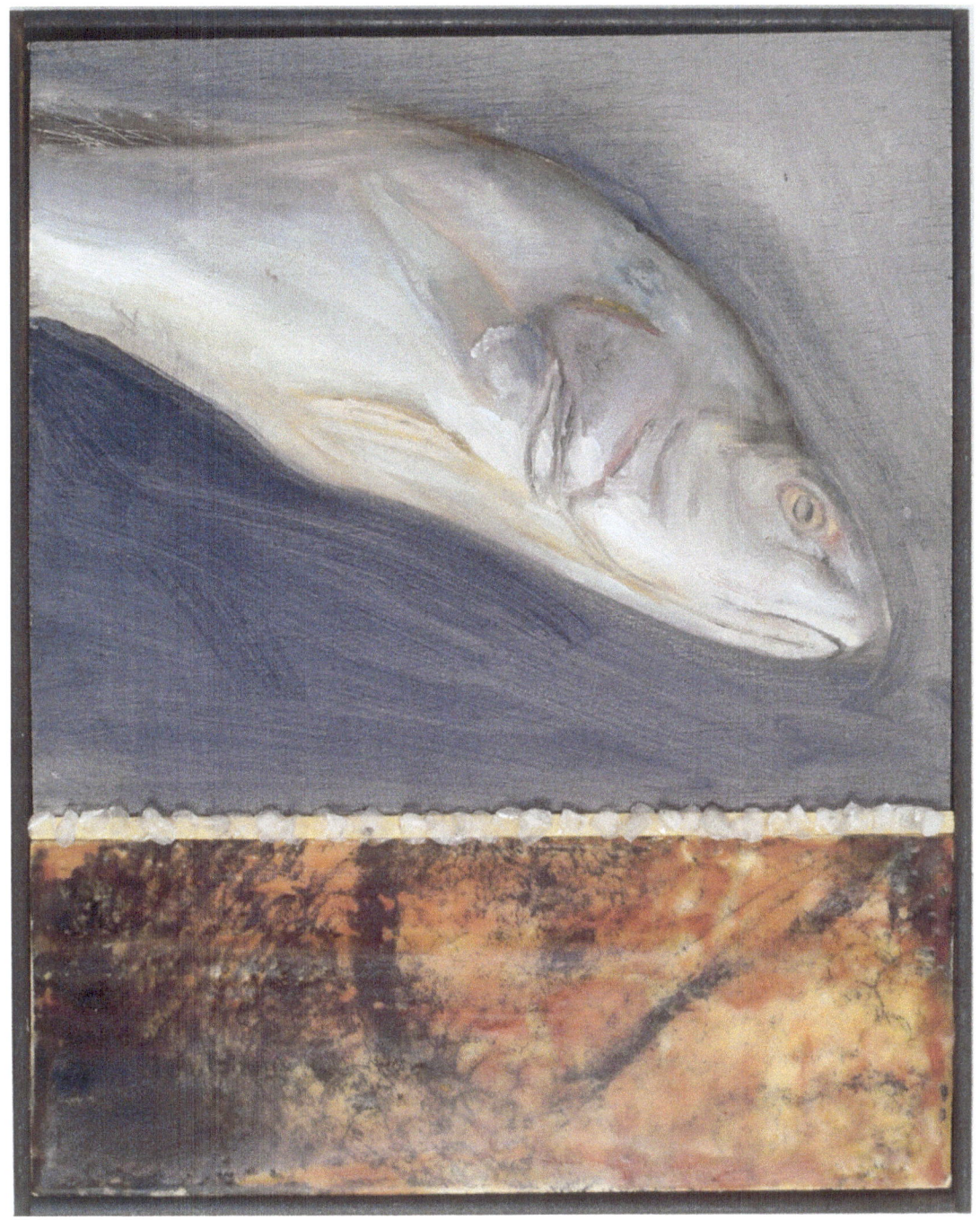

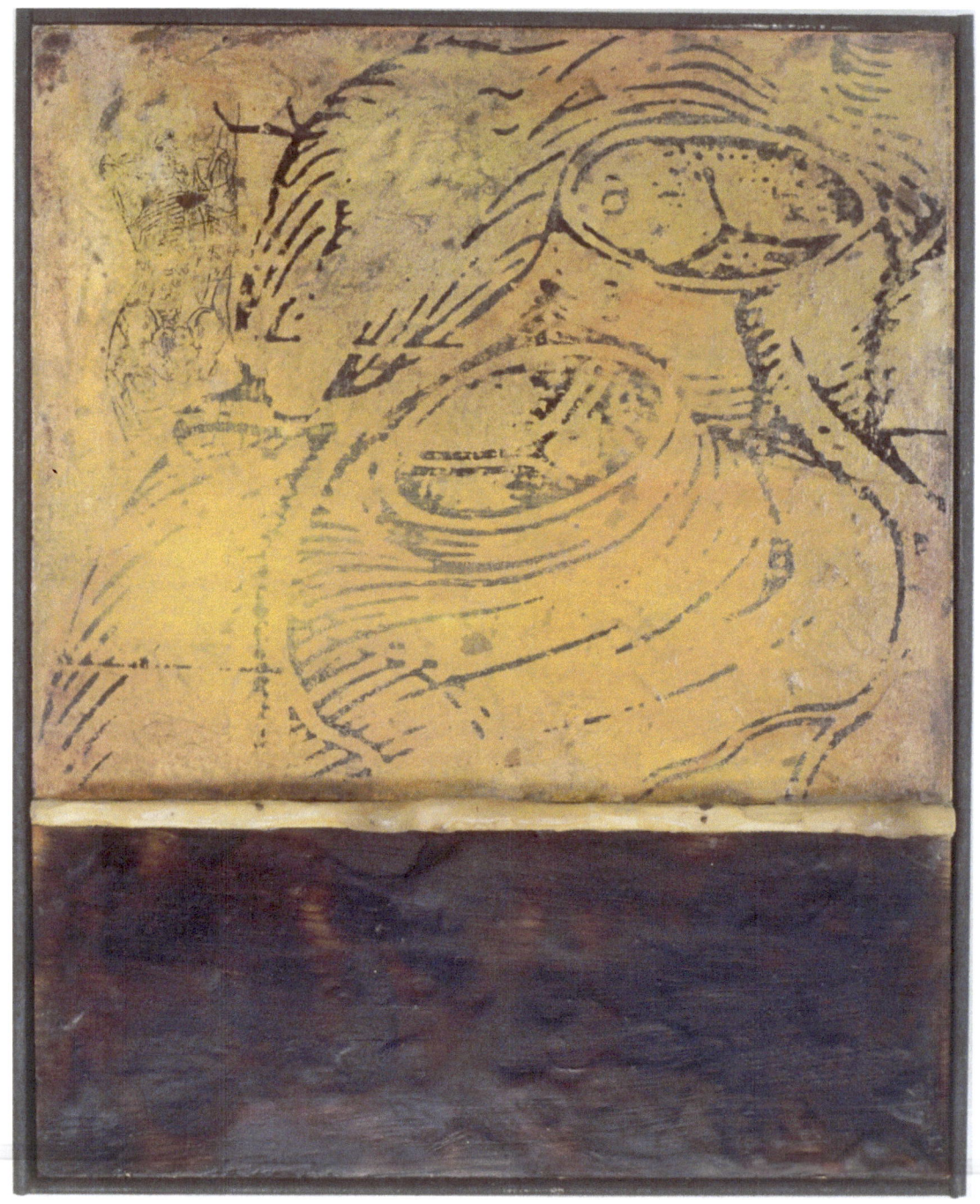

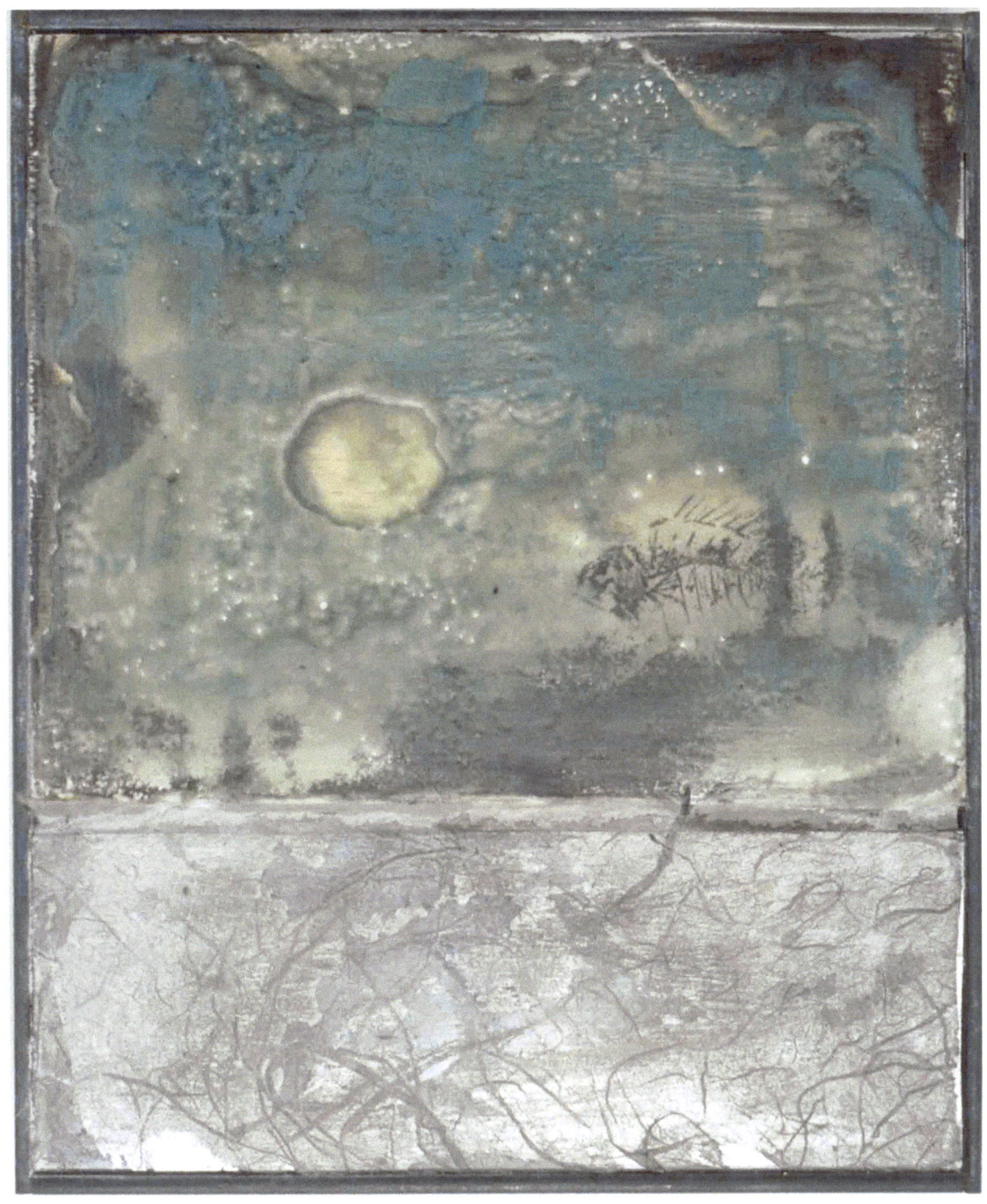

Sonya Jilani

Jinniya

For nine years of my life, I have been influenced by a character from my dreams. The character is a woman with my face, my hair, and my body, yet she is distinctly not me. She visits my dreams, giving me information that is at times helpful and at times pure gibberish. As the visits have become less and less frequent, I have started to think about her more and more. Her presence signified a time in my life when each discovery I made seemed almost psychic and I felt perfectly in tune with the universe. In each photograph or set of photographs, she is reminding me of her presence in my waking life. I equate this character to a Jinniya, a female Jinn. The Jinn are creatures in Middle Eastern mythology that, like humans, can be kind or wicked. At times, these characters visit us and impart knowledge that is helpful to our everyday lives.

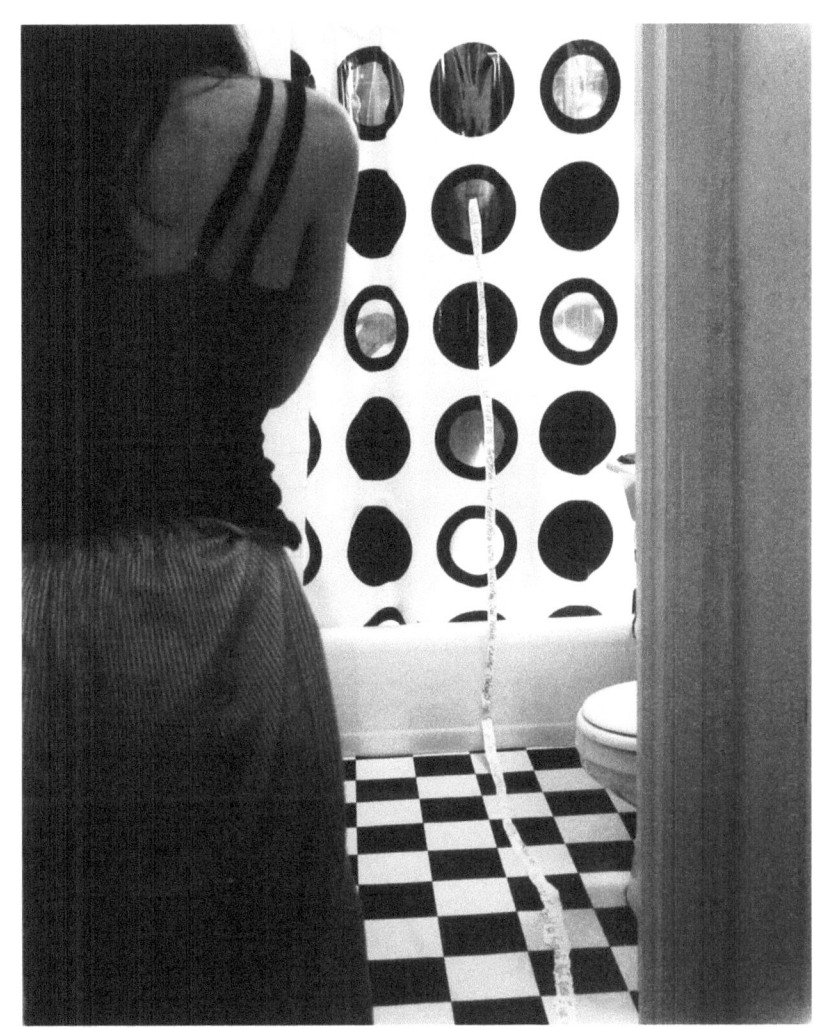

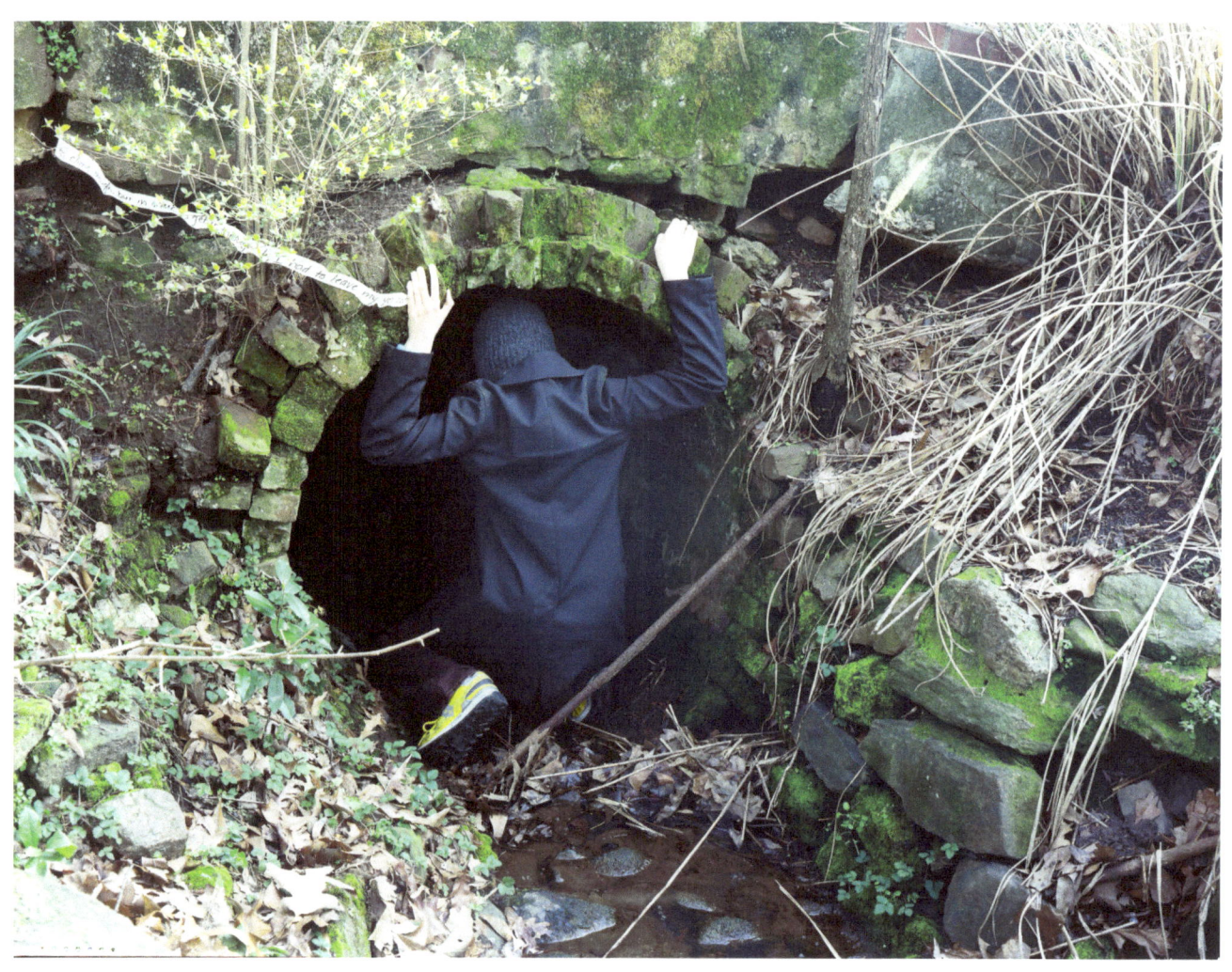

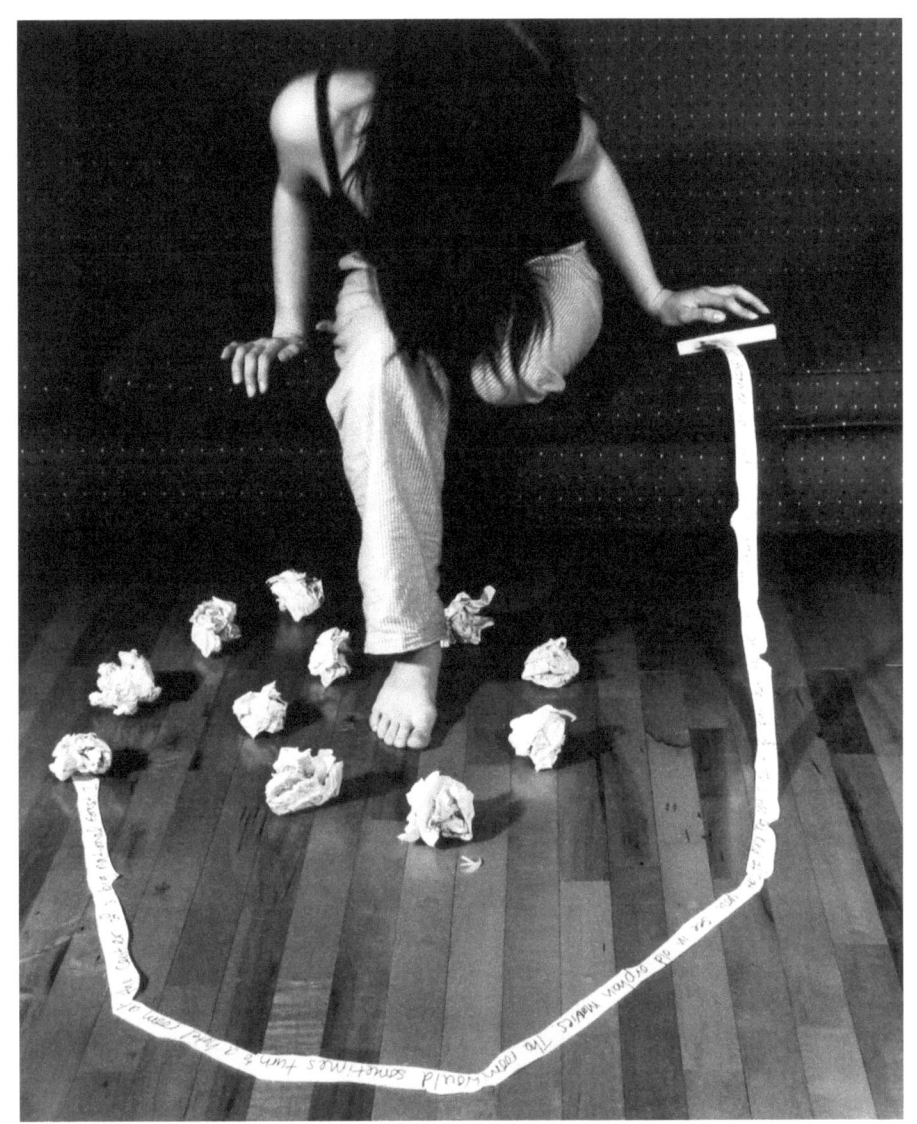

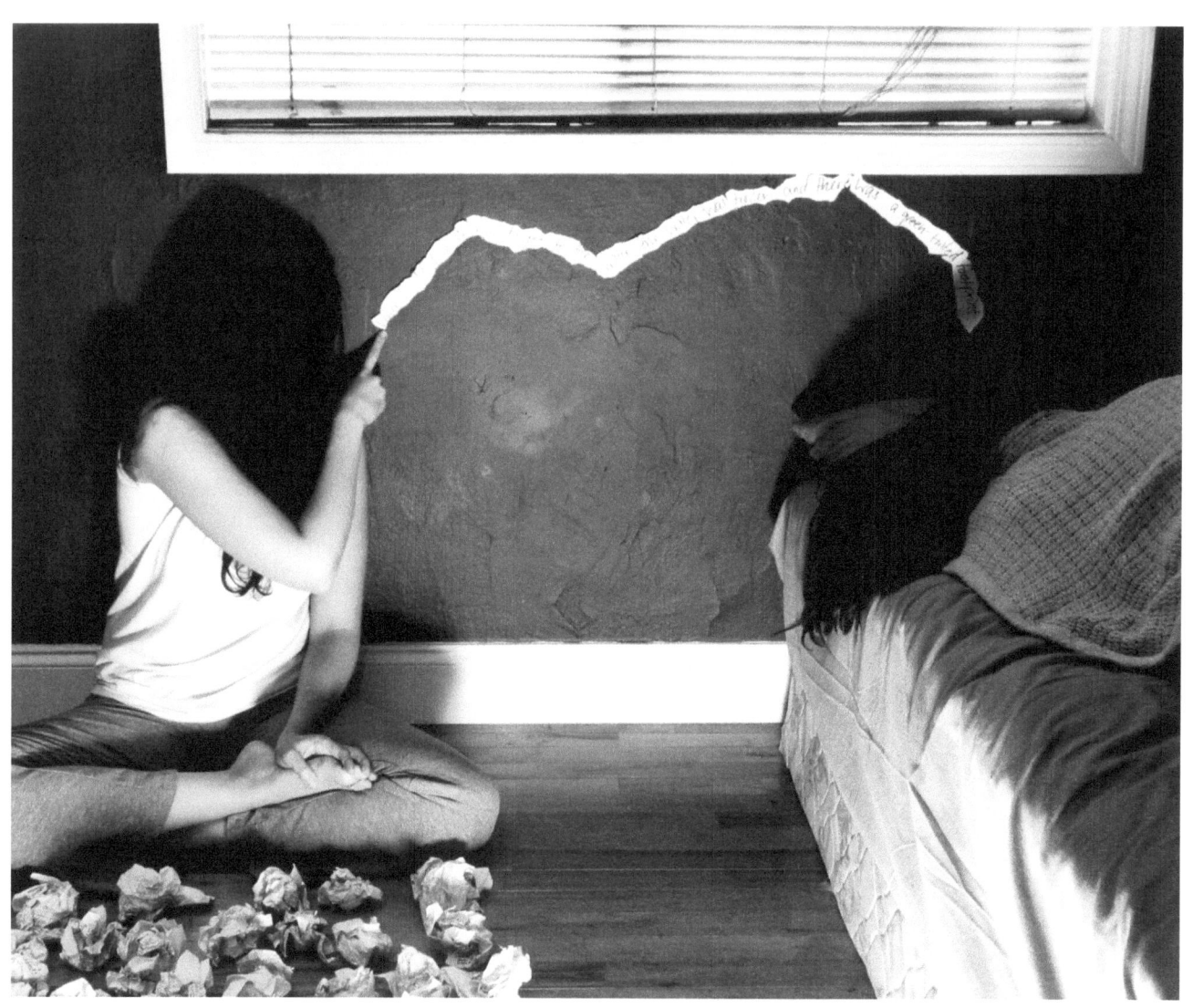

Emily Karcher

Cumming Portraits

Inspired by fashion magazine editorials, this series of images explores my continuing interest in self portraiture. These Polaroids were taken around my family's farm in Cumming Georgia; in locations I've spent years driving past, visiting, and dreaming about.

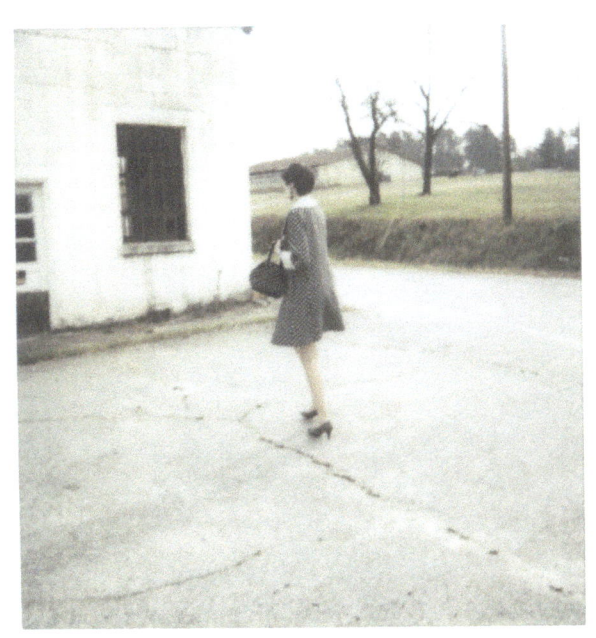

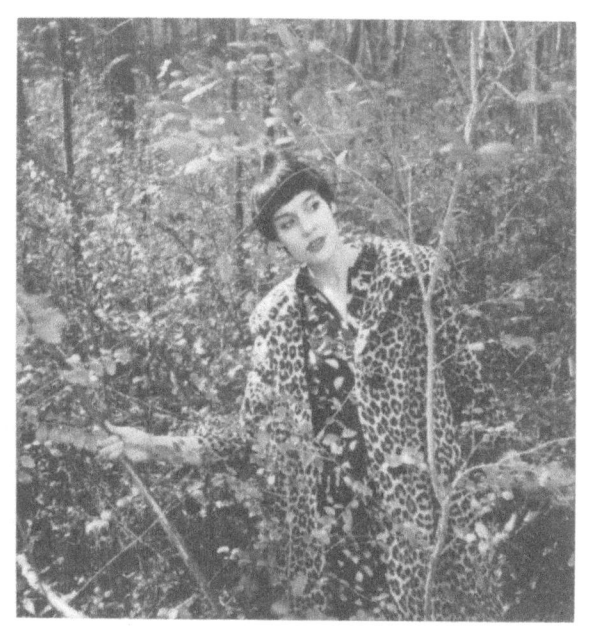

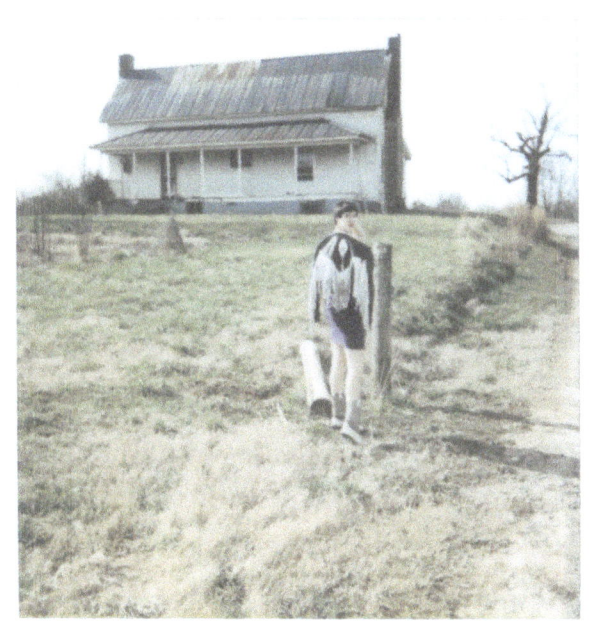

Amanda Palmer

Hysteria

(hys•te•ria) *a nervous affection in which the emotional excitability is exaggerated and the will power correspondingly diminished, so that the patient loses control over the emotions and becomes the victim of imaginary sensations.*

Guided by my dreams, I explore the tensions between the ego and the subconscious; giving into a visual hallucination while exploring the deepest truths within my life. My creations flow from dreams and surreal moments. My memory contains the judgments held within my hysteria, freedom, dream, passion, life and death. While life sometimes can be surreal, dreams somehow seem to ground me.

My past years work streams into my thinking due to false memory, confusion, and dream. All this work is a simple self-portrait. It is the closest my creation can come to what my mind sees. Explanation is worthless and dry.

The perfect piece of art is the perfect mystery, even to the artist.

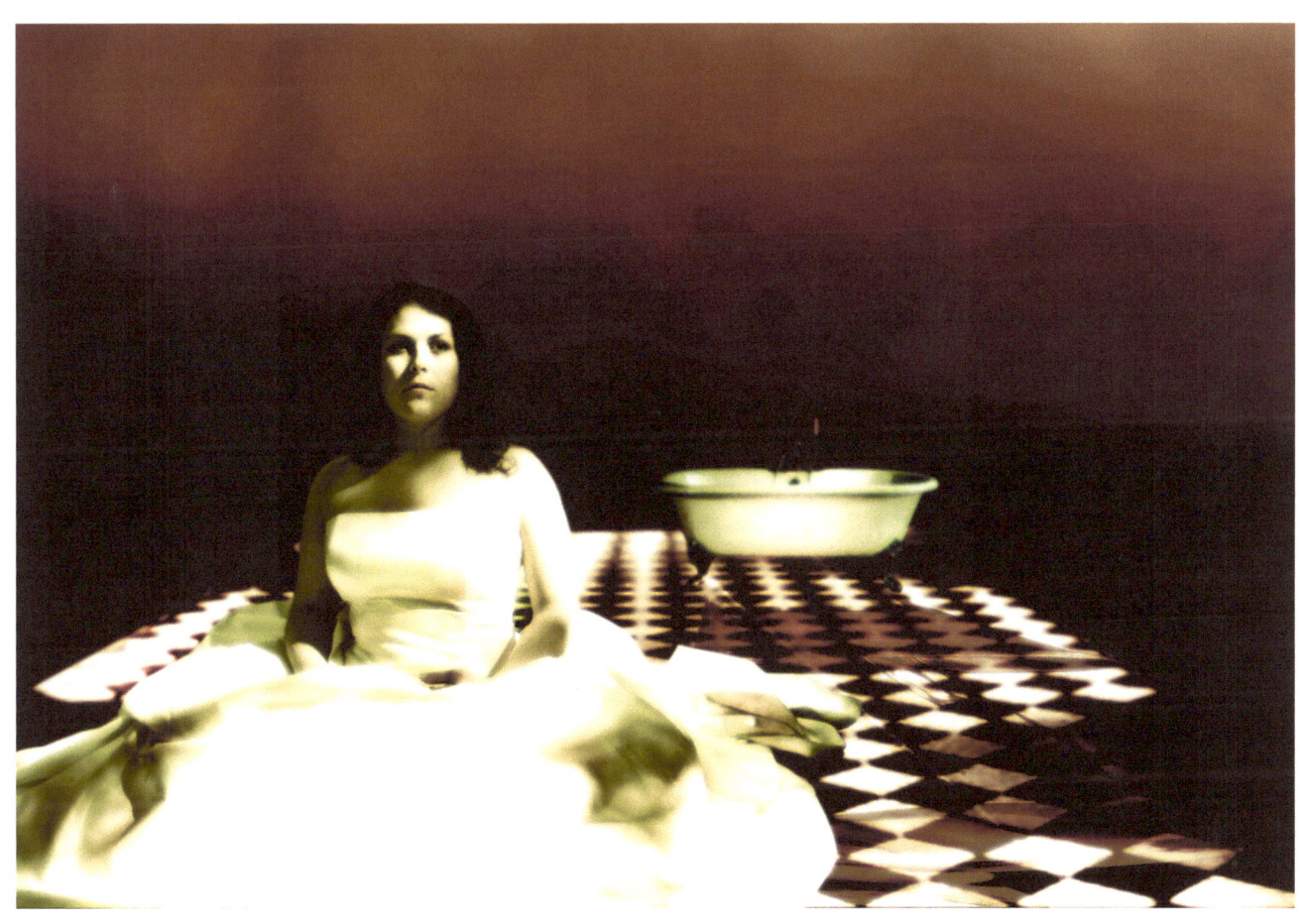

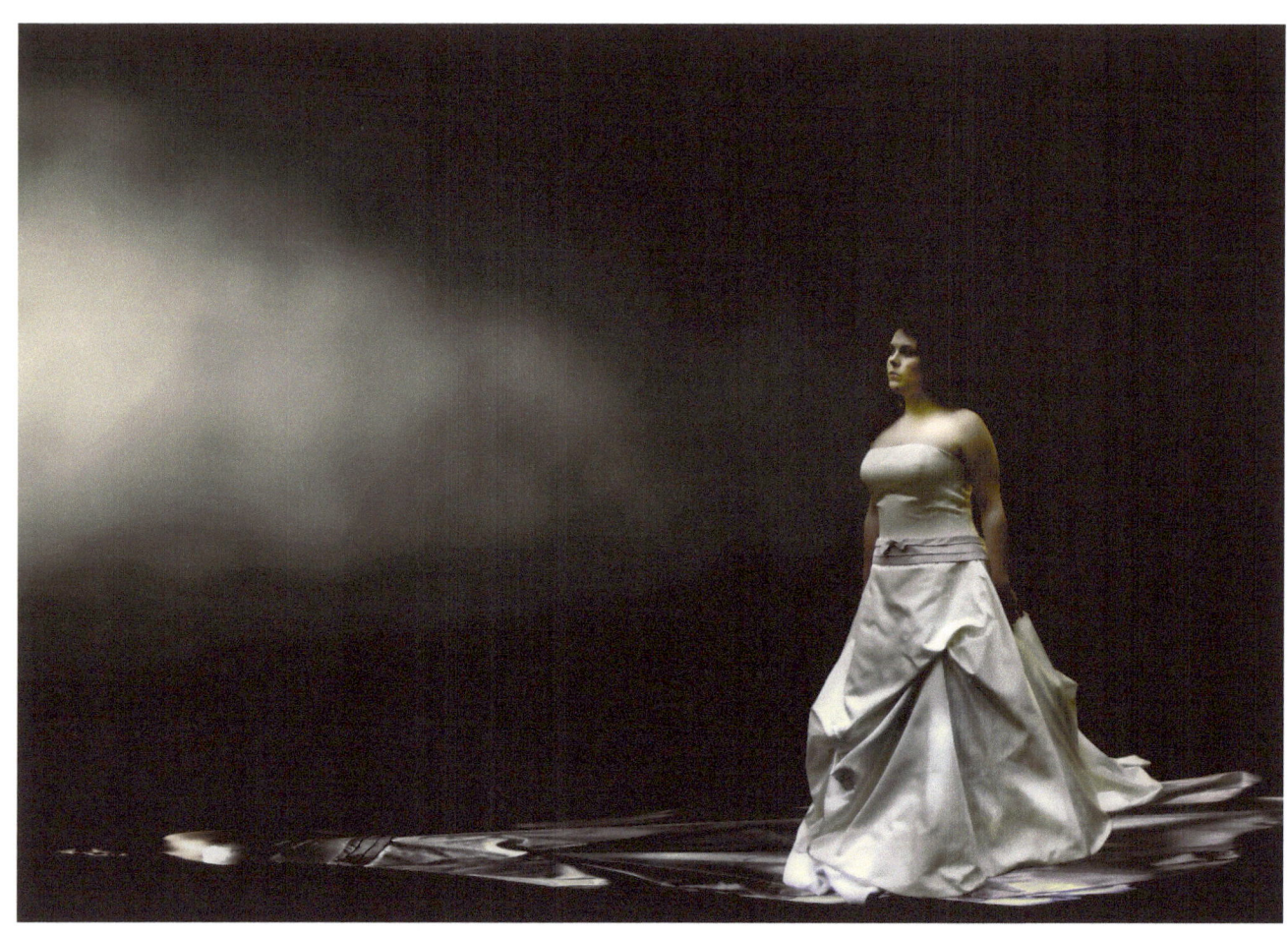

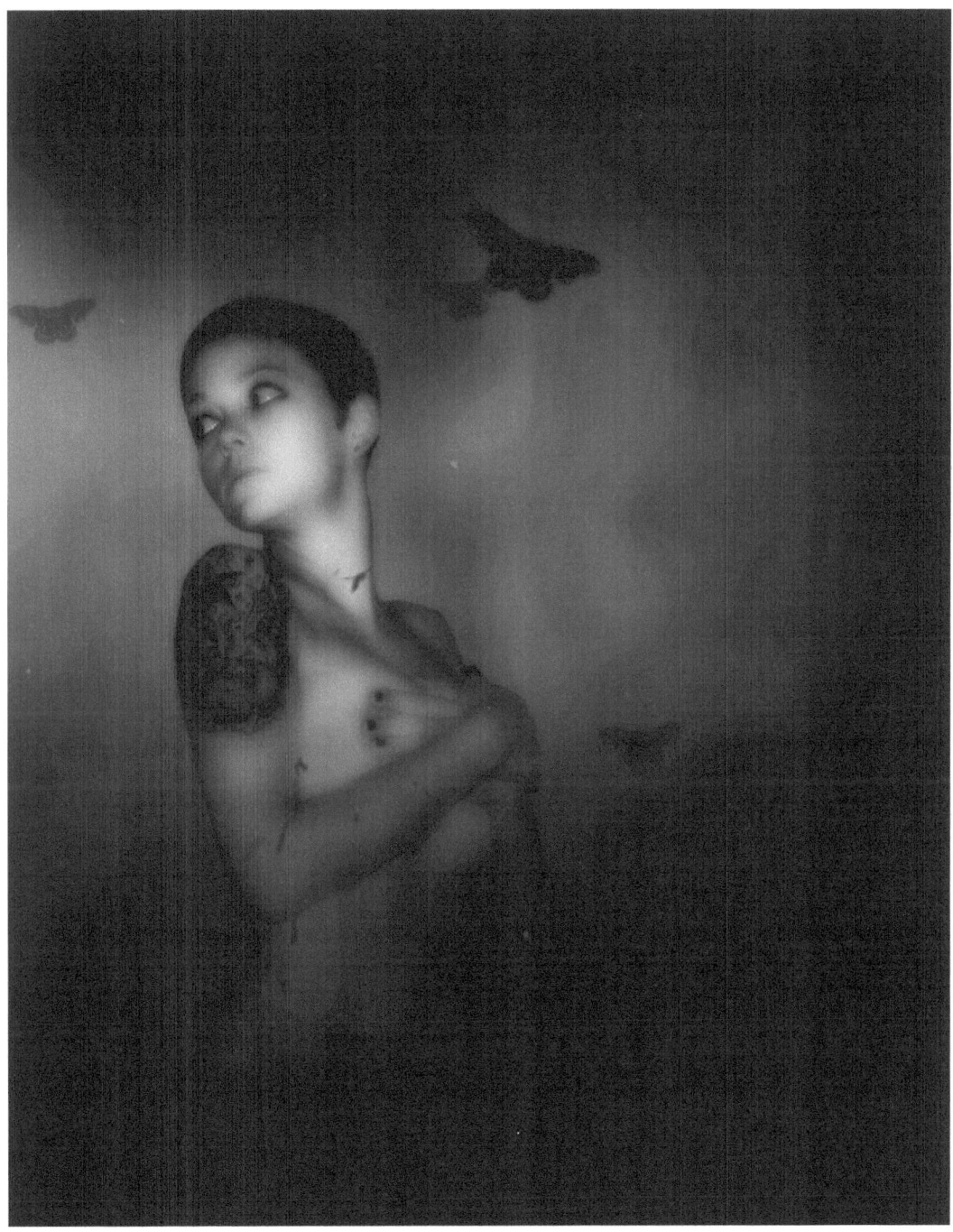

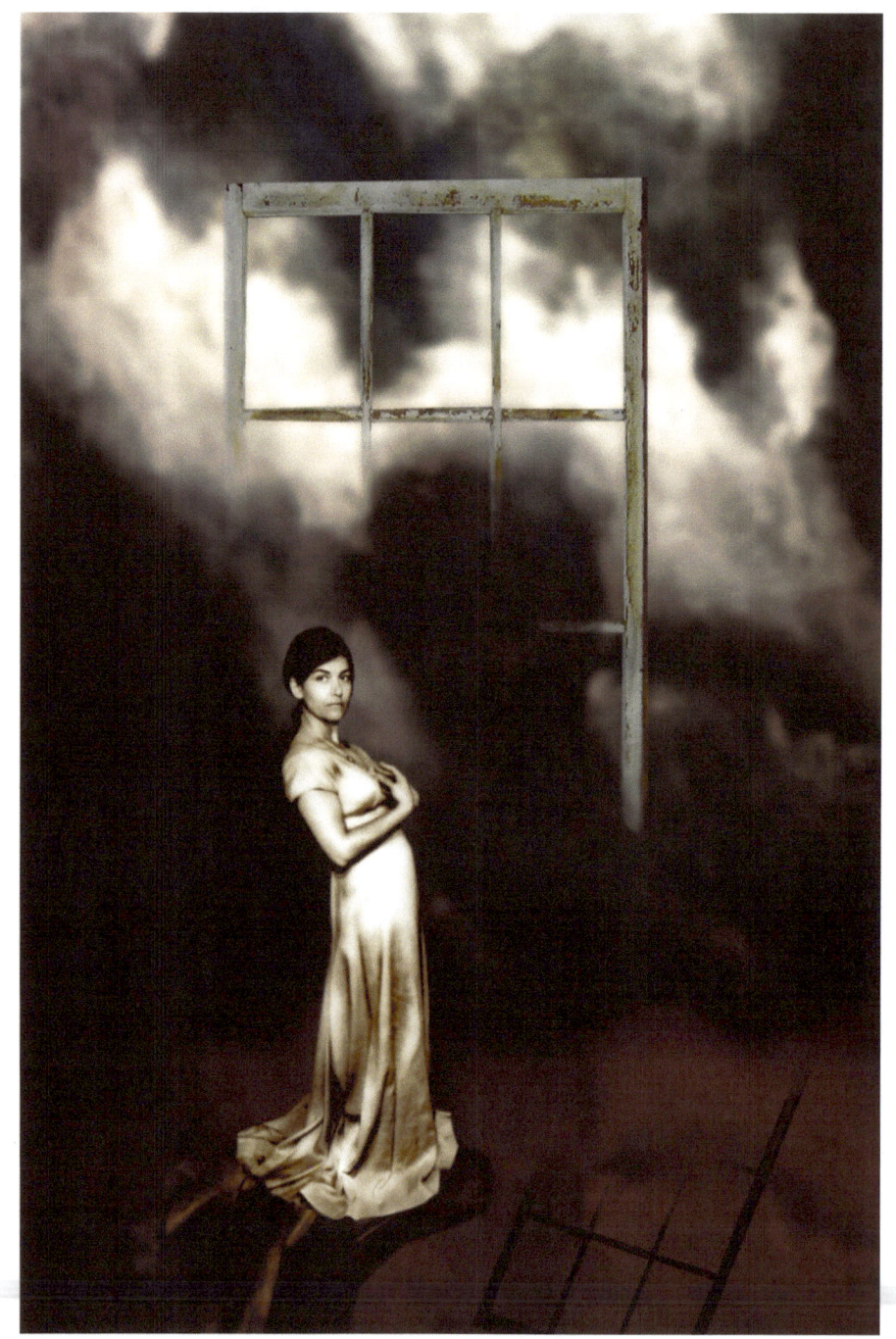

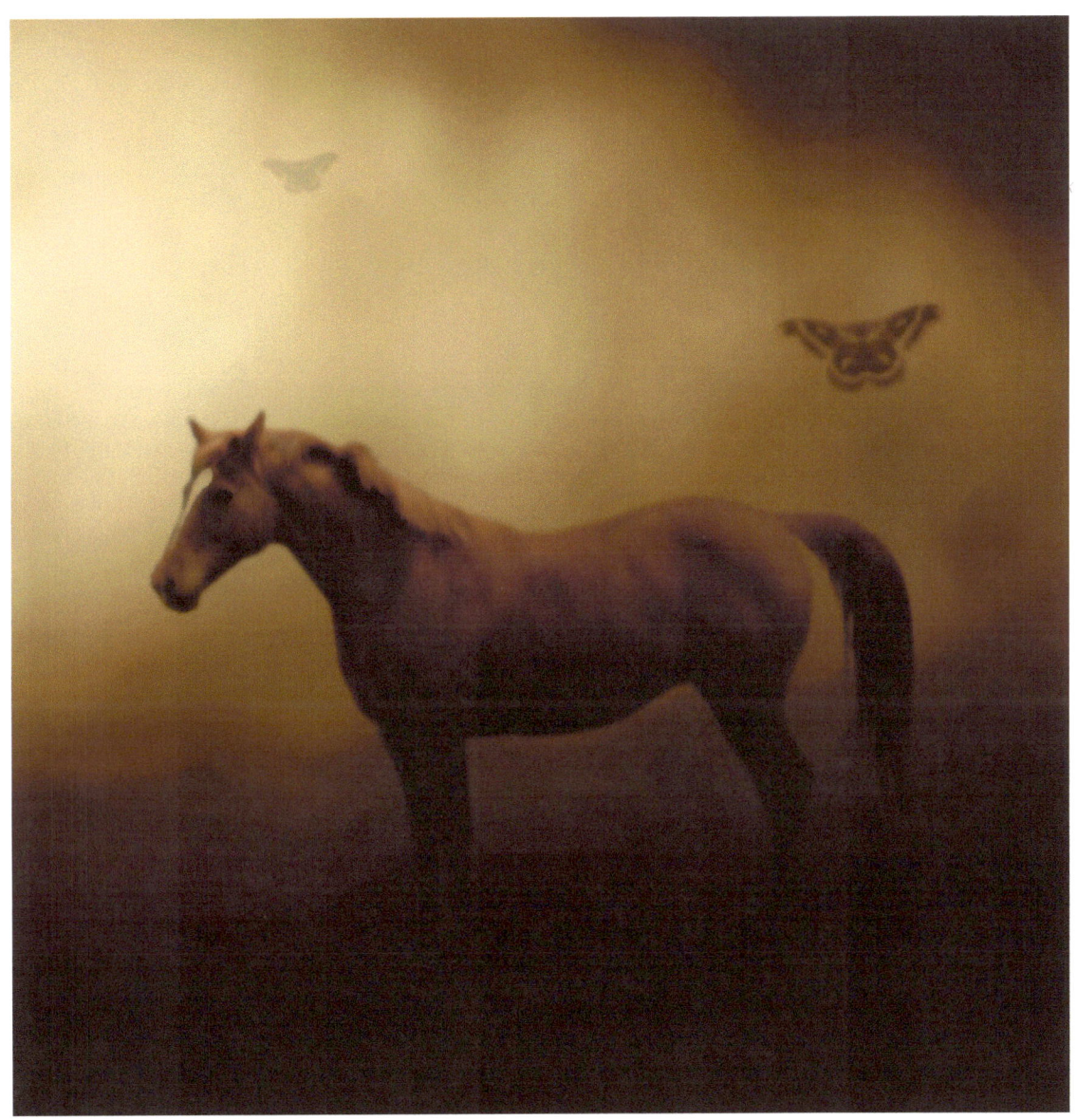

Shana Robbins

For the past several years I have been working on a series of autobiographical drawings/paintings. These paintings have evolved into performance installations, and certain performances have become paintings. Within many of the pieces, I inhabit vacant natural places containing elements or objects that hold a kind of supernatural potential. The costumes or props in these pieces are sometimes antiquated things that were used in former eras, especially by women: objects that revolt against former utilitarian and decorative expectations and take on new symbolic roles in the context of the work. Other costumes are related to the archetype of the Shape shifter-one who continually disguises and divulges how she/he appears in order to survive or to intercept lost power. Part of this survival involves camouflaging the body; merging with or disseminating into a place or space-perhaps becoming more like an animal. Another part involves assuming certain roles: cloaking or transforming the self as part of a ritualistic interaction with an atmosphere, a tree, an object, an animal, or another person. I am investigating the potential of ceremonial action to reveal something unseen and to create a sacred or healing space. Some of my performances and paintings are transparent attempts at constructing events that mirror religious or spiritual illusion, perhaps invoking numinous possibilities. I keep the atmospheres within them minimal in order to convey a potential to flourish virtually alone within these sparse, sometimes ominous environments.

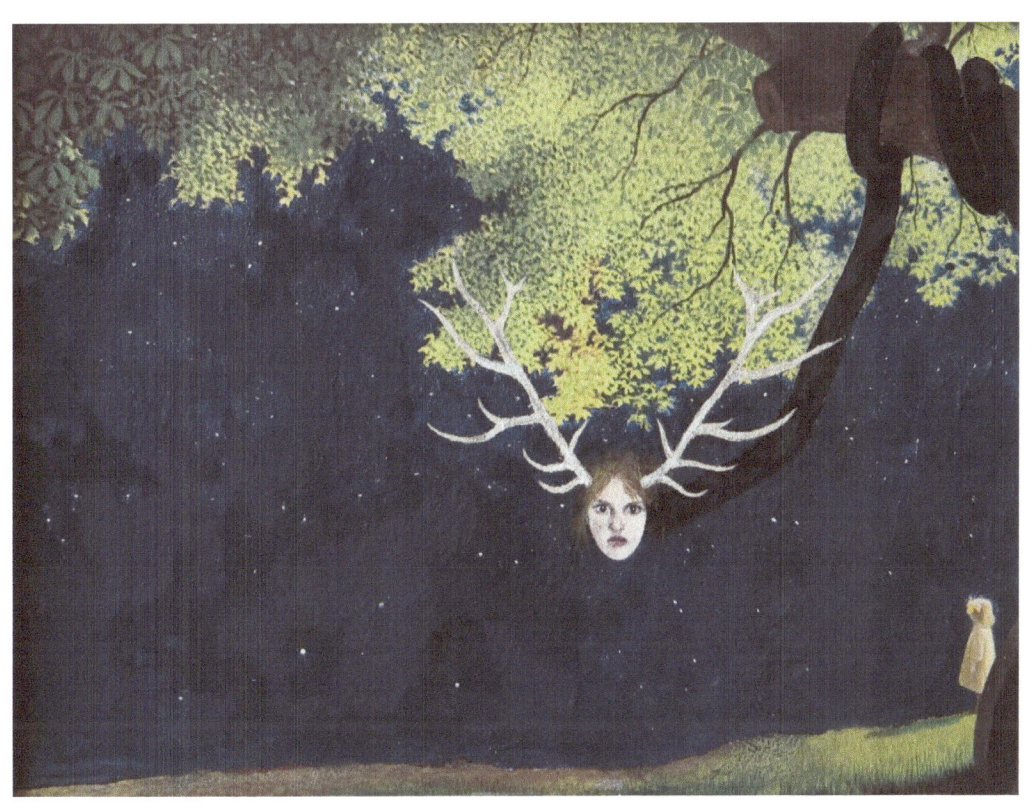

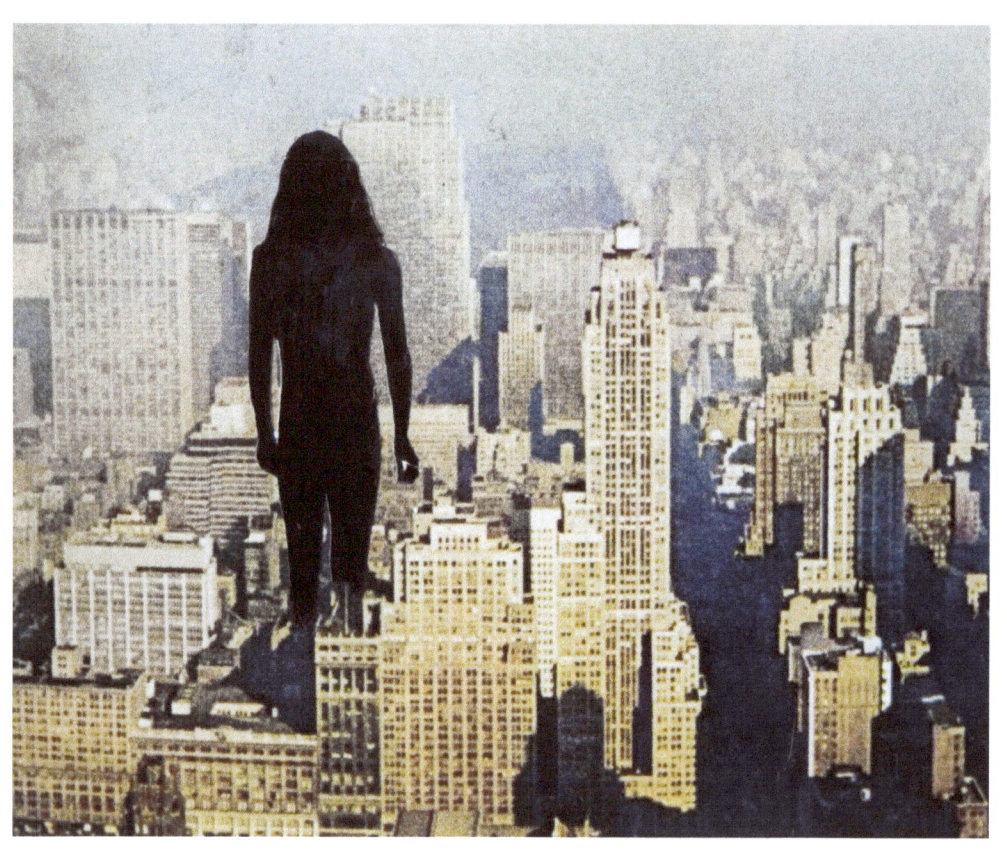

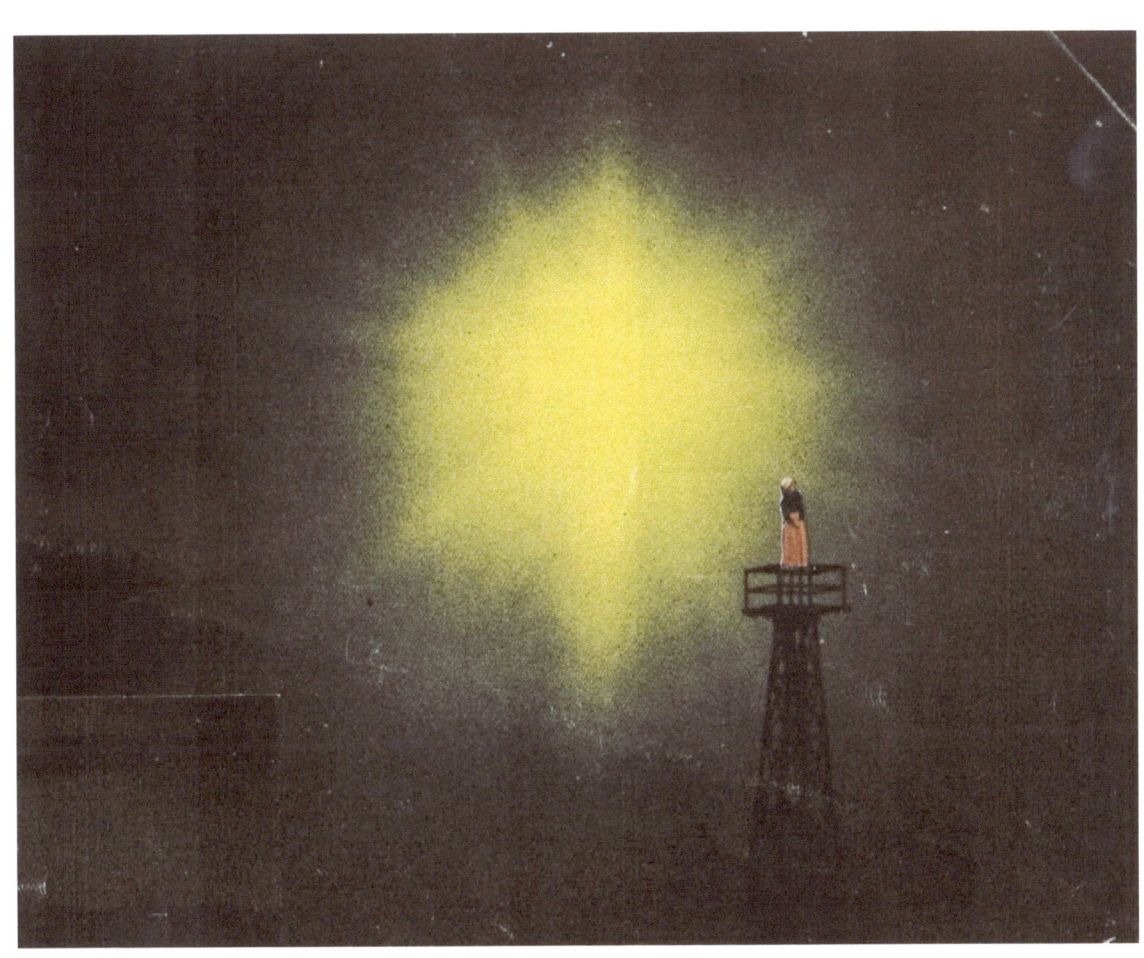

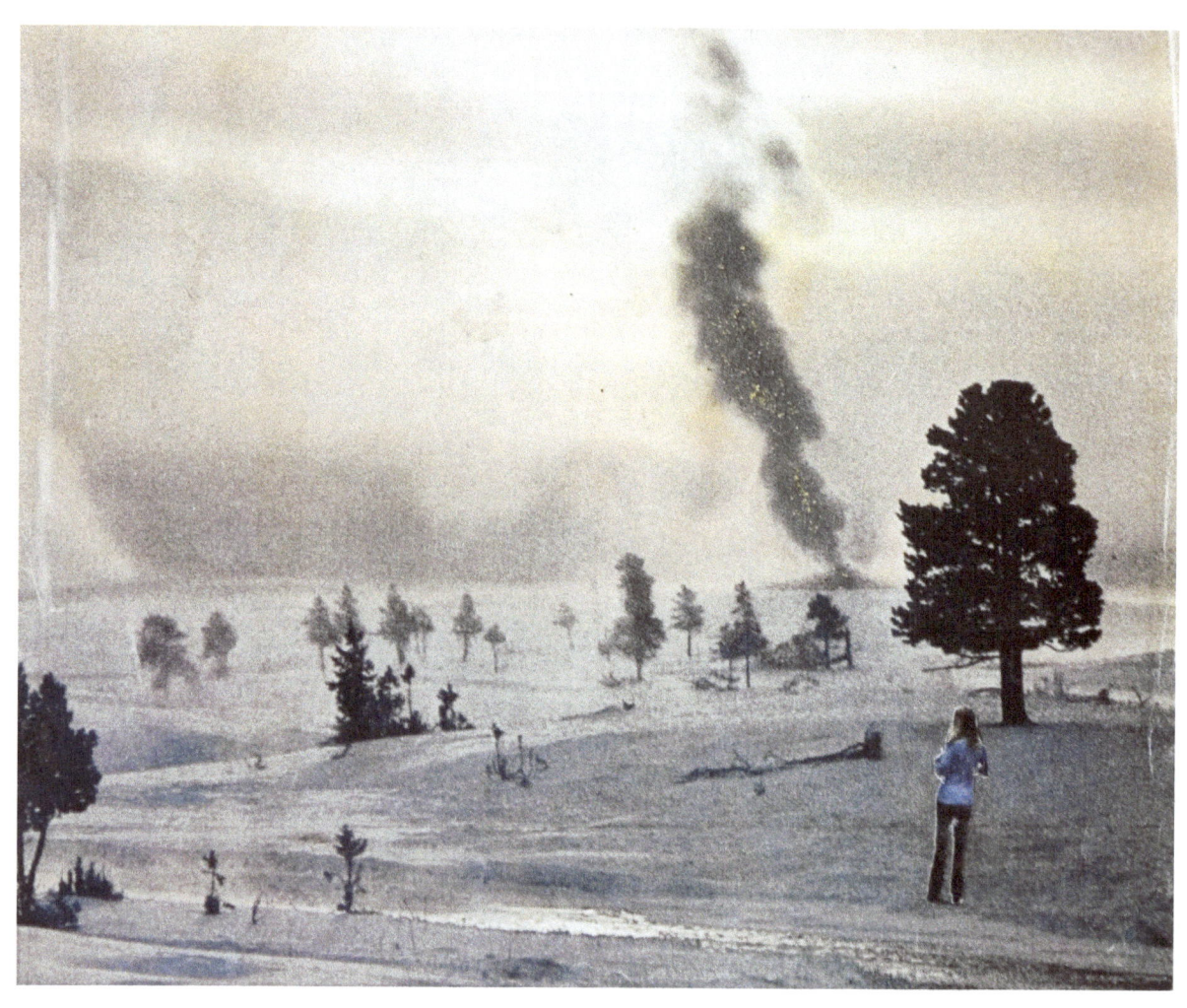

Image List

Emily Karcher

33.   *Bolton's Truck Parts 4*, 4.25" x 3.5", 2006
34.   *Jungle 4*, 4.25" x 3.5", 2006
35.   *Outsider House 1*, 4.25" x 3.5", 2006
All Polaroid photographs mounted on wood panel

Amanda Palmer

37.   *A Deck of Cards and A Jug of Wine*, 3' x 2', 2007
38.   *About the Ballroom,* 18" x 12", 2006
39.   *Everything I do Is Judged and I Mostly Got It Wrong*, 15" x 12", 2006
40.   *Remember Me Happily*, 18" x 12", 2006
41.   *The House of Self Importance*, 12" x 12", 2006
All color inkjet photographs mounted on wood panel

Shana Robbins

43.   *Anaconda Dream,* mixed media on canvas, 12" x 15", 2007
44.   *Himmer*, collage and ink on an antique book page, 7.5" x 10", 2006
45.   *Insight 34*, collage on an antique book page, 7.5" x 10", 2005
46.   *What was Left*, collage and glitter on an antique book page, 7.5" x 10", 2005

Jerry Cullum
Resume

EDUCATION: Ph.D., Graduate Institute of the Liberal Arts, Emory University, 1975. M.A., religious studies, U. of California Santa Barbara, 1970. B.A., literature, Eckerd College, 1968.

PRESENT PROFESSIONAL AFFILIATIONS: Senior editor, *Art Papers* (1996-present; associate editor, 1984-1996); freelance art reviewer, *Atlanta Journal Constitution* (since 1988); freelance curator and critic.

PUBLICATIONS: Essays in *GSD Review* (Harvard); *International Review of African-American Art*; *Journal of Architectural Education*; *boundary 2: a journal of postmodern studies*; *Raw Vision*; *Assemblage*; *Cimarron Review*; *ARTnews*; *Art in America*; *Sculpture*; *Art Papers*; *+Rosebud #4: Action* and *+Rosebud #6: Ideal* (Vienna); others; and numerous catalogue essays for individual artists and museum and university gallery shows (Montgomery Museum of Art, Georgia Museum of Art, University of Tampa, Agnes Scott College, Brenau University, others). **Reviews** in *ARTnews*; *Material Religion*; *JAAR*; *Art in America*; *Journal of Religion*; *American Ceramics*; *Christian Century*; *Sculpture*; *Soundings: A Journal of Interdisciplinary Studies*; *Religious Studies Review*; *Atlanta Journal Constitution*; others. **Poems** in *Poetry* (Chicago); *Midwest Quarterly*; *+Rosebud #5: Mystery*; *Alembic*; *Daimon*; *Garfield Lake Review*; others. Two poetry chapbooks, *Watching the Decline of Western Civilization* (Poetry Atlanta Press), *Skateboarding in Sarajevo* (Shoestring Press); self-published *Unfinished Ventures: Selected Poems 1977-2005* (lulu.com). Two CDs, *Skateboarding in Sarajevo, and other poems* (Railroad Earth) and *Sleepwalking to Kandahar* (Dharma Bums Studios). Scriptwriter, narrator, and leading actor in Carol Lafayette short video, *Skateboarding in Sarajevo*, exhibited in Rochester Film Festival, Rochester, New York; Poetry Film Festival, Berlin, Germany; other film and video festivals. Scriptwriter and actor, *Yeah, but Paradise*, multimedia performance presented by Celeste Miller in Miami, FL, Atlanta, GA and Louisville, KY.

EXHIBITIONS CURATED: for Georgia State University, Atlanta; Agnes Scott College, Decatur, GA; Georgia Perimeter College, Atlanta (co-curator Charles Nelson); Telfair Museum of Art, Savannah, GA; Marietta-Cobb Museum of Art, Marietta, GA (co-curator Cathy Byrd); Amerika Haüse, Hamburg, Berlin, Köln, München, Magdeburg, Germany, and Hatton Gallery, Newcastle upon Tyne, UK (co-curator Tina Dunkley); Arts Festival of Atlanta; other venues.

ARTWORK EXHIBITED: Oh, Those Four White Walls: The Gallery as Context (curated by Lisa Tuttle), Atlanta College of Art Gallery; Looks Good on Paper, Spruill Art Center, Atlanta; When I Was a Child, Spruill Art Center; Tickled Pink, Marcia Wood Gallery, Atlanta; Floor Fifty, IBM Tower, Atlanta; Reliable Art Show, Atlanta; Angels, Dorothy McRae Gallery, Atlanta; The Shrine Show, Emory Framing & Gallery, Atlanta; The Great Mattress Factory Exhibitions, Atlanta; various art auctions for nonprofits. Collections: Olga Viso, Lucinda Bunnen, King and Spalding Attorneys at Law, Della Patteson, others.

GUEST LECTURES DELIVERED: University of Alabama, Tuscaloosa; Auburn University, Auburn, AL; Art Museum of Western Virginia, Roanoke, VA; Alexandria Museum of Art, Alexandria, LA; University of Newcastle upon Tyne, UK; various nonprofit and private venues. Speaker on panel discussions on contemporary African art, vernacular art of the South, the artist as postmodern nomad, other topics, at Hammonds House Gallery and Resource Center of African-American Art, Atlanta; Goethe-Institut, Atlanta; Birmingham Museum of Art, Birmingham, AL; other venues.

OTHER EXPERIENCE: Co-taught introductory doctoral seminar in interdisciplinary studies, Graduate Institute of the Liberal Arts, Emory University; taught course in literature at Atlanta College of Art and delivered guest seminars in various courses there; co-taught short course for Atlanta College of Art faculty on teaching world cultures. Juried art exhibitions at University of Tennessee, Knoxville; Auburn University; University of Alabama; Art Museum of Western Virginia; other nonprofit venues including Magic City Art Connection festival, Birmingham, AL. Board member and interim director, Artists in Residence International, Atlanta. Guest editor of four issues of *Art Papers* (two in 1986, one each in 1996 and 1999) and acting editor/writers' liaison for a number of months in 1996.

Jody Fausett
Resume

Born: 1973, Jasper, GA
Education: 1994-96, Art Institute of Atlanta, Atlanta, GA

Published Work:
2003 Elemental, Tokion
2002 Contents
2001 Contents, Photo District News, Surface
2000 Surface
1998 The Photo Review
1998 Applied Arts
1997 Contents
1996 Photographers Forum

Exhibitions:
2006 Timothy Tew, Atlanta, GA "Dark Whimsey"
2005 Limelight Gallery, Atlanta, GA "KRYSTLE a performance by Shana Robbins with Jody Fausett"
        Aurora, Atlanta, GA "Photography Exhibit"
        No Space, Seattle, WA "Haut Grafix"
        Museum of Contemporary Art of Georgia, Atlanta, GA "Artist Market"
        Saved Gallery of Art and Craft, Brooklyn, NY "March Winds and April Showers"
2004 No Space, Seattle, WA "Animal Instinct"
        Museum of Contemporary Art of Georgia, Atlanta, GA "Pin-up Show"
        Disjecta, Portland, OR "…Because Cynicism Left Yesterday"
        No Space, Seattle, WA "Diamonds and Pearlz"
        King Plow Art Center, Atlanta, GA, "Hambidge Art Auction"
        No Space, Seattle, WA "Teen People"
2003 St. Helen, Brooklyn, NY "Still life and Portraits" solo   exhibition
2001 Scout, Atlanta, GA "New Work" solo exhibition
2000 Surface, New York, Chicago, Los Angeles, San   Francisco "AvantGuardian Exhibition"
        The Contemporary, Atlanta, GA "Precious: The Pathos   and Pleasure of Kitsch"
1999 Slop Brand Art, Kansas City, MO "Supermarket   Biennial"
        The Contemporary, Atlanta, GA "Biennial"
        University of Southern Illinois, Department of Motion Picture and Film, Chicago, IL "Niceville"
solo exhibition
        Art Institute of Atlanta, Atlanta, GA "Invitational"
1998 City Gallery East, Atlanta, GA "Young Eyes"
        Stare Mesto, New York, NY "The Five and Dime Show"

Lecture:
2000   High Museum of Art, Atlanta, GA "Out of the Ordinary: A Survey of Photographic Work by Atlanta-based Artists"

Other work:
2004   Saint Cecilia's Catholic School, Brooklyn, NY "The Light   Bright Project"

Articles:
2006   The Atlanta Journal-Constitution, Visual Arts, "A Gently Biting Wit" by Jerry Cullum
2004   The Daily Vanguard, Arts and Culture, Portland State University, "Art Wednesday; Cynicism Left Yesterday" by Eva Lake
       Non-Starving Artist, "Disjecta Blackmail Party Favors"
2003   Seattle Magazine, Arts and Events, "Yume Nakajima and Jody Fausett" by Sarah Greenbaum
2002   Surface Magazine, "Where are they now"
2001   BABY #2001 MGZN FOR MEDIA MODERN ARTS DESIGN, "What's up?"
1999   Art Papers, "1999 Atlanta Biennial" by Jerry Cullum

Meta Gary
Resume

Meta Gary grew up in Atlanta and attended the University of Georgia and the University of New Mexico to earn a bachelor's degree in studio art in 2003. Her work spans a wide spectrum of styles ranging from intricately planned and calculated illustrations to more intuitively loose and expressive images. She is currently living and working in Atlanta.

2007 Youngblood Gallery, Atlanta, GA
2006 Eyedrum Gallery, Atlanta, GA
2004 Passages Fine Art Gallery, Corrales, NM
2003 Lamar Dodd School of Art Gallery, Athens, GA

Heather Hartman
Resume

Education:
2005   B.F.A., Painting, Auburn University, Auburn,

Exhibitions:
2005   "Fresh Blood", Mason Murer Fine Art, Atlanta, GA
       "B.F.A. Senior Thesis Exhibition", Biggin Hall Gallery, Auburn AL
       "Auburn University Fine Arts Student Show", Biggin Hall Gallery, Auburn AL, juried
2004   "The New Aesthetes", Creations Gallery, Columbus GA
       "Auburn University Fine Arts Student Show", Biggin Hall Gallery, Auburn AL, juried
       "Pleiades", Jan Dempsey Community Arts Center,   Auburn, AL
2003   "The Human Figure in the Tradition of the Ecole Des Beaux Arts", Ravencroft School, Raleigh, North Carolina
       "Auburn University Fine Arts Student Show", Biggin Hall Gallery, Auburn, juried
2002   "Auburn University Fine Arts Student Show", Foy Gallery, Auburn, juried

Awards and Grants:
Lethander Purchase Award/ Best of Show, Auburn University Fine Arts Student Show, 2005, juried by Dr. Jerry Cullum
Lethander Award, Auburn University Fine Arts Student Show, Auburn University, 2004, juried by David Moose
Outstanding Achievement Award in Fine Art, Auburn, 2004
Wade- Sykes Scholarship Award in Art, Auburn, 2002

Sonya Jilani
Resume

Education:
2007 Bachelor of Fine Arts in Studio Art with a Concentration in Photography, Ernest G. Welch School of Art and Design, Georgia State University, Atlanta, GA

Group Exhibitions:
2006 *Smallness is a Virtue*, Aurora Coffee, Atlanta
You Have Spoken, We Are Speaking, GSU Student Center Gallery, Atlanta
Myth, Dream, Self and Story, Temple Gallery, Decatur, Georgia
Pan Terminus, Gallery 100, Woodruff Arts Center, Atlanta
Juried Student Show, Ernest G. Welch School of Art and Design Gallery, Atlanta
2005 *10th Annual Hambidge Center Art Auction*, King Plow Arts Center, Atlanta
2004 *High Five AIDS Survival Project Auction*, Ernest G. Welch School of Art and Design Gallery, Atlanta

Honors and Awards:
2001-2007 Dean's List, Georgia State University
2007 Ernest G. Welch Undergraduate in Photography Award, Ernest G. Welch School of Art and Design, Georgia State University
2006 Candidate for Larry and Gwen Walker Award, Georgia State University
Printmaking Award, Juried Student Show, Ernest G. Welch School of Art and Design, Georgia State University

Emily Karcher
Resume

Education:
2005 Bachelor of Fine Arts Degree in Studio Art, Concentration in Photography, Ernest G. Welch
School of Art and Design, Georgia State University, Atlanta, GA

2001 Summer Semester in Fashion Design, Parsons School of Design, New York, New York

2000 Summer Semester in Photography, Pratt Institute, Brooklyn, New York

Exhibitions:
2003: *Three*, Radial, Atlanta GA, Atlanta Celebrates Photography
   Annual Juried Student Exhibition, Georgia State University School of Art and Design, Atlanta
GA, Curator: Annette Cone-Skelton of MOCA GA
      Wellfair, MJQ, Atlanta GA
2004: *Annual Juried Student Exhibition*, Georgia State University School of Art and Design, Atlanta
GA, Curator: Radcliff Bailey
2007: *Eudora Welty Project*, Ernest G. Welch School of Art & Design Gallery, Georgia State
University, Atlanta GA

Bibliography:
Jerry Cullum. "GSU exhibit bears out Eudora Welty tale," *Atlanta Journal Constitution*,
February 4, 2007, p. L12.
Felicia Feaster. "See More," Creative *Loafing*, Vol. 32, NO. 24, October 23 - October 29, 2003,
p.56.

Amanda Palmer
Resume

Education:
2006 BFA in Photograph/Printmaking from Kennesaw State University

Selected Exhibitions:
2007 Ego Box, Solo Exhibition, The Blue Olive/The Catch, Marietta, Georgia
    Hysteria, Solo Exhibition, Atelier 43, Art Space International, Atlanta, Georgia,
2006 *Myth Dream Self and Story*, Temple Gallery, Curated by Jerry Cullum, Decatur, Georgia
    Hard To Swallow, Studio 1026, Atlanta, Georgia
    23rd Annual Kennesaw State University Juried Student Exhibition, Kennesaw, Georgia
    Are you Going Mental? Mental Health Association, Nuci Space, Athens, Georgia, Art Auction
2005 *First Annual Holiday Gift and Fine Art Show,* Gallery Midtown West, Atlanta Georgia
    Focus on Kennesaw, Fat Louie's, Atlanta, Georgia
    Blush, Solo Exhibition, The Blue Olive, Atlanta, Georgia
    Hollis Gillespie Book Signing, Gallery Midtown West, Atlanta Georgia
    Model of the Arts Party, Hosted by Arts Safari, Castleberry Gallery Ltd/Midtown West, Atlanta,
Georgia
Splash, Castleberry Gallery Ltd/Midtown West, Atlanta, Georgia
Paint in the Pods, The Sun Dial Restaurant, Bar & View, Atlanta, Georgia
    22nd Annual Kennesaw State University Juried Student Exhibition, Kennesaw, Georgia, First
Place in Photography
Audacity, Castleberry Gallery Ltd, Atlanta, Georgia
    Second Annual *Only Printed Matters,* Group Printmaking Exhibition, Pangea, Atlanta, Georgia
2004 *Minding Art,* benefit auction, The Five Spot, Atlanta, Georgia
Me, My-Self, Eye, The B-Complex, Atlanta, Georgia
Vice, The B-Complex, Atlanta, Georgia
    My Atlanta, Atlanta Celebrates Photography juried group photo exhibition, Piedmont Park
Bath House, Atlanta, Georgia, Winner Best in Show
Artist on The Road, Spruill Gallery, Atlanta, Georgia

Awards & Honors:
2006   Third Place in Photography, 23rd Annual Juried Student Art Exhibition, Kennesaw State
University
2005-2006 Represented artist at Gallery Midtown West, Atlanta Georgia.
2005   Glenn Hollingsworth, Jr. Memorial Scholarship, Outstanding Art Scholarship, Kennesaw
State University
2005   First Place in Photography, *22nd Annual Juried Student Art Exhibition,* Kennesaw State
University
2004   Best in Show, Atlanta Celebrates Photography, *My Atlanta*
2001   Georgia Hope Scholarship, Kennesaw State University

Reviews and Publications:

Review by Jerry Cullum in the AJC, Access Atlanta "Dreamscape's stark imagery", Thursday, Jan.25, 2007

Review by Jerry Cullum in The Atlanta Journal-Constitution, "Spunky work christens hip new gallery", Sunday, May 1, 2005

Publication in Share Magazine, Kennesaw State University, Volume 34 Issue 1, 2005

Article and **Interview** in Flourish Magazine, the College Of the Arts Kennesaw State University, Volume 3, Number 1, Summer 2005

Article and **Interview** in The Sentinel, Kennesaw State University, Wednesday, March 23, 2005

Shana Robbins
Resume

Education:
2007 MFA Candidate, Georgia State University
2005 Bachelor of Fine Arts (BFA), Atlanta College of Art, Atlanta

Awards:
2007 Joseph Perrin Award for artistic merit
2006 Winnie G. Chandler Scholarship for artistic development
2005 Winnie G. Chandler Scholarship for artistic development
2004 Hambidge Center Fellow
1995 Merit Scholarship, Atlanta College of Art

Selected Exhibitions and Performances:
2006 *EarTrumpet*, Performance installation for ARTperforms series, Eyedrum Gallery, Atlanta
 Dark Whimsy, Timothy Tew Gallery, Atlanta
 Rainbow Machine and Drawing Voices, performance installation series and exhibition of drawings, Ernest G Welch School of Art and Design Gallery, Georgia State University, Atlanta
 Body *Double*, Performance and exhibition of paintings, No Space Gallery, Seattle, Washington
 Performance within Pam Longobardi's installation *Sky is Fallen*, Sandler Hudson Gallery, Atlanta
 Myth, Dream, Self, and Story, Temple Gallery, Atlanta
2005 *March Winds and April Showers*, Saved Gallery of Art and Craft, Brooklyn, NY
Haute Grafix, No Space Gallery, Seattle, Washington
 Krystle, Performance installation in collaboration with Craig Dongoski and the M.U.T.E.D, Limelight Gallery, Atlanta
 Women's Caucus for Art National Juried Exhibition: *Gender in Motion*, 3Ten Haustudio, Atlanta
Little Things Mean a Lot, The Swan Coach House Gallery, Atlanta
 Refusing to Dance Backwards, Spruill Gallery, Atlanta
2004 *Made at ACA*, Juror: Trevor Smith from the New Museum of Contemporary Art, NY, Atlanta College of Art Gallery
 All is Not Lost, solo exhibition, Gallery 100, Woodruff Arts Center, Atlanta
 By Myself, The Swan Coach House Gallery, Atlanta
 I Dare You, solo exhibition, Garage Projects, Atlanta
2001 *Cream*, Space 1180, Atlanta
2000 *Simple Pleasures*, 290 Martin Luther King Loft, Atlanta
1999 Vanessa Beecroft performance, Chelsea Piers, New York
 The Fire Show, City Hall East Gallery, Atlanta 1998 *Investigation, Initiation, Exploration, Celebration, Penetration: A Journey into Lifestyle, Eroticism, and Imagery,* Old Lake Claire Baptist Church Space, Atlanta

1997   *The November Project*, Old Lake Claire Baptist Church   Space, Atlanta

Selected Bibliography:
FOX, Catherine, "World of Good," in *The Atlanta Journal-Constitution*, 12/30/2006
CULLUM, Jerry, "A Gently Biting Wit" in *The Atlanta Journal-Constitution*, 10/22/2006
Atlanta magazine, "Portrait of the Artists," April 2005 (photo feature)
Art Papers magazine, page 69, July/August 2005 (reproduction)
FEASTER, Felicia, "Get it, Give it!" in *Creative Loafing*, November 24, 2005. page 47
FOX, Catherine, "A Look within reveals truths about us all" in The Atlanta Journal-Constitution, August 29, 2004
FEASTER, Felicia, "Women Behaving Boldly" in *Creative Loafing*, August 19,2004
LACE, Candy, "Laid Bare on Canvas..." in *Jezebel Magazine*, September 2004
BYRD, Cathy, "Whipped Cream" in *Creative Loafing*, March 28, 2001
New York Times Magazine, Vanessa Beecroft performance photo, November 14, 1999
WRIGHT, Matt, "Private Collections" in The Scene, February 21, 1998
BYRD, Cathy, "Praying for Sheetrock" in *Creative Loafing*, November 22,1997

About StudioSwan

StudioSwan is the combined studios, gallery and home of nationally accredited artists Tom Swanston and Gail Foster. In 2005 they joined over three dozen families to start Serenbe, a new "Live, Work, Play" community in south Atlanta. StudioSwan is located in the heart of the Serenbe hamlet at the center of looping country roads and well-worn footpaths that make walking easier than getting into a car. A community of homes, gardens, public farms, bike paths and horse trails, Serenbe has the authentic look of a village built over time and yet encourages architectural diversity.

StudioSwan, the gallery, exhibits a select group of distinguished artists from across the United States. Like Tom and Gail this exclusive group of artists share powerful and eloquent visions supported by a highly advanced mastery of their media.

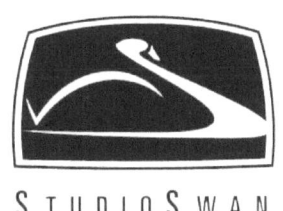

STUDIOSWAN

Serenbe · 9077 Selborne Lane · Palmetto · Georgia 30268 · (770)463-9440 · www.studioswan.com